secrets of
COMPANION PLANTING

secrets of
COMPANION PLANTING

plants that help, plants that hurt.

Brenda Little

LEATHERWOOD
PRESS

Silverleaf Press Books are available exclusively
through Independent Publishers Group.

For details write or telephone
Independent Publishers Group
814 North Franklin St.
Chicago, IL 60610
(312) 337-0747

Silverleaf Press
8160 South Highland Drive
Sandy, Utah 84093

Contents

Introduction

1. What Is Companion Planting?

2. Designing a Companion Garden

3. Managing Insects and Pests with Companion Plants

4. A to Z Guide to Companion Plants

5. Good Companions / Bad Companions

6. Maintaining a Companion Garden

Introduction

Many hints in this book come from my grandfather, a happy man and an unorthodox gardener. His cabbages squeaked with health, his beans snapped with a crack, and a person needed a bib to eat one of his apples. "Nature isn't tidy," he used to say, loading us up with flowers and veggies all picked from the same patch. You never saw bare soil in his garden. He believed in crowding his plants together, and he never purchased a garden spray in his life. Only recently did I realize what a wise old bird he was. Simply put, he had the good sense to work with nature instead of against it.

It would be unreasonable to claim that practicing companion planting and following the hints in this book will produce a wholly pest- and trouble-free garden. However, as you incorporate these inexpensive ideas into your own gardening philosophies, at least you will be doing no harm. Hopefully, this is enough to encourage you to try things out.

In all things of nature there is
something of the marvelous.

~Aristotle

....

chapter 1

What Is Companion Planting?

Companion planting is not a concrete science, but people have gardened for a long time, and they've noticed things. When tomatoes and potatoes are planted close together for three years in a row and produce poor tomatoes and marble-size potatoes, then produce bumper crops the fourth year when planted at opposite ends of the garden, something clicks. The gardener might not know the reason, but he or she can certainly see the results.

Companion planting has been practiced for thousands of years. The ancient Romans

and Greeks noted that crops such as olives and grapes grew better when planted together, and tropical indigenous cultures have grown integrated companion-planted gardens for generations.

Early European settlers and explorers to the Americas noted the natives' practice of growing corn and pumpkins together and corn with beans. These companionships are still standard practice. Perhaps best known are the friendship between basil and tomatoes and the antipathy between onions and legumes.

The practice of companion planting is another way to imitate the benefits from models found in nature. For those who pine for scientific reasons as to why plants can make good or bad neighbors, it has a lot to do with exhalations, scents, and root excretions. And there's no accounting for tastes; plants can prefer strange bedfellows. A delightful humorist once put her finger right on it. "Contentment," she said, "is a matter of who is with whom." That's what companion planting is all about.

Following is a list of several ways in which companion planting can benefit individual plants in the garden:

Flavor Enhancement: Some plants, especially herbs, have a tendency to subtly change the flavor of other plants around them.

Hedged Investment: Sowing many plants in the same space increases the odds of some yield, even if one category encounters problems.

Level Interaction: Plants that grow on different levels in the same space can provide ground cover or work as a trellis for other plants.

Nitrogen Fixation: Plants that fix nitrogen in the ground can make nitrogen available to other plants.

Pest Suppression: Certain plants can repel insects, plants, or other pests through their biochemicals.

Positive Hosting: Some plants attract or are inhabited by insects or other organisms that benefit the plants. Ladybugs and mantids are examples of beneficial insects.

Protective Shelter: Some plants can serve as a windbreak or as shade from the afternoon sun for other plants.

Trap Cropping: Certain plants can attract pests to keep them away from other plants.

Through all these different methods, companion planting works with nature's balance in the environment. Companion gardeners learn to understand this balance as they practice arranging and designing the plants in their garden in the most optimal ways. Ultimately, companion gardening will work for those who take the time and make the effort to figure out what works best for their garden.

There are no gardening mistakes,
only experiments.

~Janet Kilburn Phillips

....

chapter 2

Designing a
Companion Garden

I n designing a companion garden, it
is the placement of plants in relation
to one another that is important, not
the shape and size of the garden. If you
plan a companion garden on paper before
sowing the seeds, you will save yourself a
great deal of confusion and frustration.

To plan a companion garden on
paper, first make two columns. In the left
column, list the plants you wish to grow.
In the right column, list their companions.
Choose companions that are suitable for

the space available in the garden. Sketch a personal garden plan that works with the plants you wish to grow, your type of soil and climate, the availability of sun, etc. Be creative. Through trial and error, you will learn what works best for your garden.

Success in a brand-new companion garden may be minimal. Sometimes a full cycle (all four seasons) may pass before you see signs of progress. And sometimes certain years just turn out better than others. As you gain experience, you will understand your garden and what works best for each individual plant and its environment.

The following rotation has been designed for gardeners who have only a small amount of space. It is based on a standard three-bed system and has been developed to take advantage of complementary height, space, and nutrient requirements.

Three-Bed, Five-Year Rotation

This rotation does not include potatoes or herbs. Potatoes should be grown in separate plots because they usually come up twice as thick the summer following their first harvest. Some herbs favor certain vegetables but not others. The small-space gardener can grow herbs in large plastic tubs, with two or three companion herbs to each tub. Move these around the different beds to suit different crops as they grow.

Bed 1

May 1
tomatoes (sl)
celery (sl)
parsnip (sd)

November 1
brassicas (sd)
onions (or sd)
garlic (sg)

July 1
carrots (sd)
lettuce (sl)
Swiss chard (sl)

February 1
peas (sd)
parsley (sl)

June 1
tomatoes (sl)
beans (sd)
lettuce (sl)

November 1
oats or rye (sd gm)

May 1
corn (sl)
squash (sd)
peas (sd)

November 1
brassicas (sl)
onions (sl)

June 1
carrots (sd)
lettuce (sl)
Swiss chard (sl)

November 1
carrots (sd)
broad beans (sd)

June 1
tomatoes (sl)
celery (sl)
parsnip (sd)

Repeat, bringing plantings forward by
one month for second cycle of five years.

Planting Legend
sl = seedling
sd = seed
sg = segment
gm = green manure

Bed 2

March 1
peas (sd)
carrots (sd)
lettuce (sl)

July 1
tomatoes (sl)
celery (sl)
leeks (sd)

January 1
cabbage (sl)
leeks (sl)

June 1
corn (sl)
beans (sd)
cucumber (sd)

December 1
rye (gm)

Repeat, bringing plantings forward by
one month for second cycle of five years

May 1
peas (sd)
carrots (sd)
lettuce (sl)

October 1
broccoli (sl)
Brussels sprouts (sl)
garlic (sg)

April 1
carrots (sd)
garlic (sg)

August 1
lettuce (sl)
beets (sd)
cauliflower (sl)

April 1
peas (sd)
carrots (sd)

August 1
beans (sd)
corn (sl)

November 1
Swiss chard (sl)
onions (sl)

June 1
tomatoes (sl)
celery (sl)

Planting Legend
sl = seedling
sd = seed
sg = segment
gm = green manure

Bed 3

April 1
corn (sl)
cucumber (sd)
beans (sd)

October 1
cauliflower (sl)
broad beans (sd)
Swiss chard (sl)

May 1
tomatoes (sl)
celery (sl)
carrots (sd)

October 1
Brussels sprouts (sl)
broccoli (sl)
onions (sl)

May 1
beets (sd)
parsnip (sd)
onions (sl)

September 1
cabbage (sl)
cauliflower (sl)
parsnip (prev.)

March 1
peas (sd)
carrots (sd)
lettuce (sl)

July 1
tomato (sl)
carrots (sd)
cabbage (sl)

December 1
broad beans (sd)
winter lettuce (sl)

June 1
corn (sl)
beans (sd)

Repeat in second cycle.

Planting Legend

sl = seedling
sd = seed
sg = segment
gm = green manure

Companion Crops

SUMMER GROUPING 1

All seedlings planted May 1.

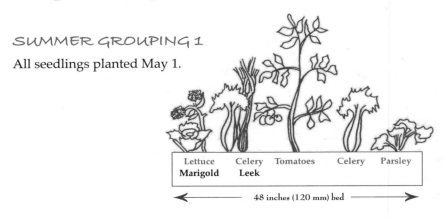

| Lettuce | Celery | Tomatoes | Celery | Parsley |
| **Marigold** | **Leek** | | | |

← 48 inches (120 mm) bed →

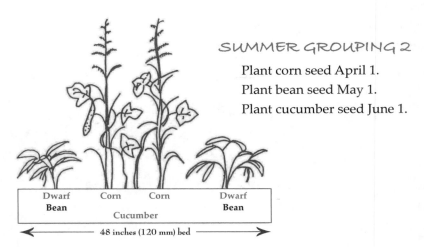

SUMMER GROUPING 2

Plant corn seed April 1.
Plant bean seed May 1.
Plant cucumber seed June 1.

Dwarf	Corn	Corn	Dwarf
Bean			**Bean**
	Cucumber		

← 48 inches (120 mm) bed →

AUTUMN GROUPING

Sow carrot seed
September 1.
Plant cabbage / cauliflower
seedlings September 1.
Plant garlic segments.

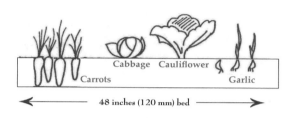

Cabbage   Cauliflower

Carrots   Garlic

48 inches (120 mm) bed

WINTER GROUPING

Plant broad-bean seeds
October 1.
Plant brassica and Swiss chard
seedlings October 1

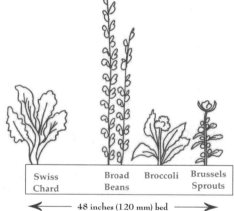

| Swiss Chard | Broad Beans | Broccoli | Brussels Sprouts |

48 inches (120 mm) bed

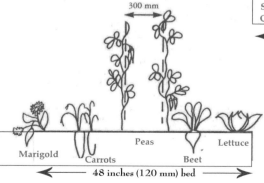

Trellis
300 mm

Marigold   Carrots   Peas   Beet   Lettuce

48 inches (120 mm) bed

SPRING GROUPING

Sow pea seeds February 1.
Sow carrot, beet seeds March 1.
Plant lettuce seedlings March 1.

Herbs and Friends

VEGETABLE	FAVORED HERBS	UNWELCOME HERBS
asparagus	parsley, basil, marigold, rue, wormwood	dill, fennel
beans	petunia, rosemary, summer savory	fennel, rue, wormwood
beets	summer savory, chamomile	fennel
brassicas	mint, dill, chamomile, nasturtium, sage, peppermint, rosemary, southernwood, thyme	fennel
carrots, parsnips	rosemary, chamomile, sage, chives , wormwood, flax, summer savory	dill, fennel
celery	sage, rosemary	lovage

VEGETABLE	FAVORED HERBS	UNWELCOME HERBS
corn	purslane, tansy, lamb's quarters, nasturtium, borage, sow thistle	sage, fennel
cucurbits	borage, nasturtium, tansy	sage, fennel
lettuce	tagetes, marigold, lovage	fennel, dill
peas	petunia, marigold, lovage	fennel, dill, rue
potatoes	nettle, flax, marigold, horseradish, pigweed	garlic, rosemary
tomatoes	basil, parsley, beebalm, borage, mint, calendula, marigold	rue, wormwood

*No occupation is so delightful to
me as the culture of the earth, and
no culture comparable to that of
the garden.*

~Thomas Jefferson

. . . .

chapter 3

Managing Insects and Pests with Companion Plants

ANTS

"Go to the ant, thou sluggard; consider her ways and be wise." The biblical exhortation must have saved the life of many an ant.

But while ants may be industrious, they also protect aphids, one of the greatest enemies of the garden. Ants love "honey dew," the sweet substance produced by aphids, and they go to great lengths to look after their "milking herds." They carry aphids from plant to plant and thereby spread viral disease throughout the garden. Ants also protect other insects whose secretions are tasty but which damage plants the gardener is attempting to grow. The interests of the ant and the gardener do not coincide.

If you still cannot bring yourself to exterminate these earnest little workers, you can at least discourage them. Ants won't go near plants with bonemeal sprinkled around them. Ants also stay away from plants protected by cut-off plastic milk cartons.

Ants hate the scents given off by tansy, pennyroyal, and southernwood. A patch of these pleasant, pungent plants by the back door will prevent ants from crossing the threshold. Place sprays of these herbs, either fresh or dried, on larder shelves, and ants that have gotten in will make a hasty exit.

Ants

If you have become exasperated enough to actually kill the ants, spray their nests with pyrethrum or garlic laced with white pepper.

APHIDS

Plant lice—commonly known as aphids—are easy to see and destroy. They can be green, yellow, black, or red. Aphids parasite most cultivated plants and are known by the name of the plant they attack—rose aphids, citrus aphids, carrot aphids, strawberry aphids, etc. The black variety attacks the growing shoots of the broad bean.

Aphids do not like orange-colored nasturtiums. You may not like them either, but if you grow a border of them around a bed of plants you wish to protect, you can use the seeds, pickled, instead of capers.

Aphids puncture a plant and suck its sap. While doing so, aphids give off a sticky substance that rapidly molds and makes the plant look messy. As explained earlier, this "honey dew" is an ant delicacy, and ants will nursemaid the aphids in order to ensure their food supply. In carrying aphids from plant to plant, ants help spread viral disease.

The finger and thumb method of killing both aphids and ants is easy but tedious and messy. A strong blast of cold water on aphid-ridden plants will clear many of the pests away. A soapy-water spray followed by a rinse with clean water is even better. "Tea" made from garlic, nettles, basil, or wormwood (see "Herb Teas" for preparation methods) and used as a spray is the best of the lot. Planting clumps of these same herbs near plants you wish to protect will also make the area less attractive to aphids.

If you meet a ladybug in the garden, coax it to your aphid-ridden plants. It will eat about four hundred of the pests in a week.

If driven to buy a commercial spray, stick with pyrethrum or nicotine—these sprays kill on contact and do no further harm.

ASSASSIN BUGS

Stay your hand if you see a brown insect that looks like a praying mantis

Assassin Bug

and has long wings. This is an assassin bug, and it eats caterpillars, aphids, and leafhoppers. Assassin bugs stab their victims, paralyzing them with toxic saliva, then suck them dry. Don't panic if you should happen to get stung; damage will be slight though temporarily painful.

BEES

Bees do a good job of plant pollination, so it makes good sense to attract them to your garden. Bees love lavender, fennel, lemon balm, basil, coriander, thyme, and borage.

BEETLES

Many people kill beetles on sight. Some black and brown shield-shaped beetles have the sense to keep out of the way during the day and come out at night to feed on snails and caterpillars. If one has got his timing wrong, give him a chance to get back into hiding.

Some beetles feed on snails and caterpillars.

BIRDS

Birds are the gardener's ally quite as often as they are his enemy. They rely on insects for up to 50% of their diet and will feed on them in preference to anything else.

A gardener will always find himself in a quandary when it comes to birds. It is each gardener's personal choice whether to encourage or discourage these beautiful creatures.

BUTTERFLIES

Like birds, butterflies can be problematic in a garden. Most butterflies do not harm plants and may even aid in pollination, but their larvae are a different matter. Caterpillars eat the leaves, shoots, flowers, and roots of plants. The pleasure of seeing the beautiful gauzy-winged adults hovering above the flowers will have to be paid for later.

Butterfly

CATERPILLARS

Pepper sprinkled on dew-wet leaves will protect them from the predation of caterpillars. Infestations of caterpillars can be stopped by spraying with garlic tea (see Herb Teas) laced with pepper.

CENTIPEDES

Centipedes, which are ginger-colored and have one pair of legs to every body segment, are useful because they live on decaying garden stuff, not growing matter.

Centipedes are useful.

CUTWORMS

Cutworms have smooth, fleshy bodies and can be any color from cream through green and gray to black. They feed on the stems of young plants, eating right through them so that the plants collapse. Cutworms are fond of young flower seedlings, cabbage, cauliflower, beans, and sweet corn. Tansy is a

Cutworms are dangerous in the garden.

good deterrent. If you have no tansy growing where cutworms are active, bruise a few shoots and leaves of the plant and strew it around the area, or squeeze tansy juice on your fingers and gently smear it on the stems of the young plants you wish to protect.

DAMSELFLY

This insect, which can be distinguished from the dragonfly by the way the wings are folded down when the body is at rest, is equipped like the praying mantis and the assassin bug, with forelegs that are ideal for catching aphids and disposing of insect larvae. Leave it be.

Damselfly

DRAGONFLIES

If you see any dragonflies in your garden, don't spray them. Dragonflies seize and kill other flying insects that could be nuisances to you and your plants.

Dragonflies are certainly no nuisance to the gardener.

Earthworm

EARTHWORM

Earthworms are very important to the well-being of garden soil. They help aerate the soil by burrowing channels that allow air and water to penetrate the earth. They also deposit mineral-rich castings along their trail. Add them to your compost heap to increase the rate of decomposition. Earthworms also help by eating eelworms.

EARWIGS

An earwig looks like a beetle but can be distinguished by its long, narrow body and the pincers at the posterior end of its abdomen. Rather than getting in your ear, earwigs come out at night and make a mess of your plants.

An old, broken garden hose can be put to good use as

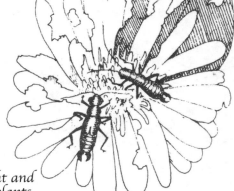

Earwigs come out at night and make a mess of your plants.

an earwig trap. Cut the hose into small pieces and scatter them around the garden to provide an attractive shelter for these pests. Then collect the hose pieces and dispose of them. Hollow bamboo stems will do just as well. Even an old coat left out overnight will collected earwigs for dispatch the following morning.

EELWORMS

These microscopic pests, called nematodes, attack both the roots and stems of plants, weakening them significantly. Eelworms don't like marigolds. Many other pests don't like marigolds either, which makes these flowers a must for a border around your vegetable garden.

If you think eelworms have been attacking above ground, boil a cup of sugar in water to dissolve it. Then dilute the mixture and spray it on the plants you wish to protect.

FLEAS

Fennel. Fennel and yet again, fennel.

FLIES

Pots of basil, tansy, or eau-de-cologne mint (or all three) placed in strategic positions will keep the housefly away from the house. Such pots are also useful in barbecue areas.

Flies

FROGS

A pond in the garden will attract frogs. Though they may keep you awake at night with their croaking, they will also do a good job for you. Frogs eat many garden pests, particularly egg-laying adults who could prove much more of a nuisance than the frogs.

FRUIT FLY

The fruit fly is a dreadful pest. Tansy, basil, and southernwood planted around peach and apricot trees, and any others subject to fruit flies' depredations, will be helpful. But it's no use pretending they will be enough to keep the fruit safe!

The fruit fly is a dreaded pest.

GECKO

You are lucky if you have a gecko in your garden. These small lizards hide during the day and come out at night to feed on insects. If you turn over loose bark and find him, let him rest.

HOVERFLIES

A hoverfly looks like a tiny wasp but is silent as it hovers above plants. A hoverfly is a gardener's friend, as members of its family eat mealybugs, grasshoppers, aphids, and aphid larvae.

LACEWINGS

These small green insects with four gauzy wings and golden eyes are often seen at night fluttering around an outside light. Their larvae are called "aphid-lions" because of their voracious appetite for the pests. Lacewings lay their eggs on the topside of leaves and can easily be recognized by the thread-like stalk by which they are attached to the leaf. If you leave them be, the eggs will hatch, and the larvae, equipped with magnificent jaws, will

Lacewing

run down the thread, immediately on the attack for their first meal. They suck the body juices of the aphids and then use the empty skins to camouflage themselves. They also eat moth eggs, caterpillars, mealybugs, scale insects, and thrips.

LADYBUGS

"Ladybird, ladybird, fly away home, Your house is on fire and your children all gone." I can't imagine how the nursery rhyme originated, for even in early times the ladybug was a welcome visitor. Their name is a corruption of "Our Lady's bird," a name given by grateful peasants when a sudden swarm of one of the species arrived providentially and cleared up an infestation of pests that were devastating the vineyards.

Ladybugs down an incredible number of aphids in a week but also enjoy scale insects, mealy bugs, leafhoppers, whiteflies, mites, potato beetles, and bean beetles. Ladybugs penetrate areas

The ladybug is a gardener's best insect friend.

of plants that are inaccessible to spray, and they are the gardener's most useful insect friend. Most people can recognize adult ladybugs by their red, yellow, or orange shells with black spots or stripes. But the small, spiky, torpedo-shaped larvae are often mistaken for pests when they are actually attacking and eating pests.

*Lizards patrol the garden and keep down snails,
grasshoppers, and beetles.*

LIZARDS

Happy is the garden with lizards in it. Some lizards look fierce,
but most are not. If your dog's hackles rise when confronted with
one, take him away and let the lizard escape. Lizards patrol the
garden and keep down snails, grasshoppers, and beetles. Even if
they did no good at all, the sight of a lizard on the path, soaking up
the sun, is reward enough.

MEALYBUGS

Mealybugs suck the life out of plants, but fortunately they are one
of the ladybug's favorite foods. A spray with soapy water and a scrape-
off with a knife is recommended by many experts. But a brush soaked
in methylated spirits applied direct to the pests, though a tedious
exercise, is not only satisfying but highly effective.

MICE

Mice are fond of pea seeds and bean seeds. If you roll the seeds in paraffin before planting, these rodents will leave them alone.

Mice also enjoy melons and bulbs. Make sure you grow plants nearby that mice don't like, such as catmint, chamomile, corn, dwarf elder, everlasting pea, sea onions (squill), spearmint, and spurges.

MILLIPEDES

Millipedes may look creepy, but they do no harm. They live on decaying matter and do a good job cleaning up.

MOSQUITOES

Mosquitoes can be kept out of the house by pots of basil, pennyroyal, mint, southernwood, or tansy placed on windowsills and near outside doors. Bruise the leaves and rub them on your skin to repel mosquitoes from you.

MOTHS

Stinging nettles, violets, spurge, lilac, and elder are all attractive to several species of moths, so they can be used as a trap crop to lure moths from the plants you don't want them near.

Moth

Such predators as praying mantis, lacewings, earwigs, assassin bugs, and certain birds will eat moth larvae. Moths are deterred by plants like celery, rosemary, sage, tansy, thyme, peppermint, and dill.

The cabbage moth is kept away by dill planted in the vicinity, and the clothes moth by mint or lavender sachets in the wardrobe and drawers. And dried citrus peels are a good moth repellent for both clothes and food.

PRAYING MANTIS

The praying mantis is a rather frightening-looking insect. It is also one of the most ferocious creatures on earth, and it attacks practically anything that moves. The mantis seizes its prey between its forelegs and rips it apart with its powerful jaws. Beetles, spiders, aphids, caterpillars, leafhoppers,

The praying mantis—a useful killer.

bugs, and other mantis (or even your finger if you are unwary enough to tease a mantis) can all fall victim. The mantis doesn't just kill garden pests; it kills beneficent insects too. But it can be useful, so subdue the instinct to kill it on sight. You may have seen a brown, lumpy mass as big as an egg attached to a leaf or twig. These are eggs laid by the female praying mantis, and they will hatch in the spring.

RED SPIDER MITE

Red spider mites—so tiny that even an infestation is hard to spot with the naked eye—love dry and dusty conditions. They work on the underside of leaves, sucking the sap, and their presence is betrayed by a mottling, stippling, and silvering of the leaf. A soap and water spray, with particular attention paid to the underside of all the leaves, will help. Better still, keep the red spider mite at bay by misting your plants in dry weather.

ROBBER FLY

This ugly, ferocious fly catches other flying insects and squirts them with saliva to immobilize them, then sucks out their body juices. The robber fly does some good for the gardener, but it's up to you how you treat the bug.

SCALE

A strong spraying with soapy water is an initial method of attack against scale. Always use soap and not detergent (see "Soap"). Rinse with clear water after spraying and be prepared to repeat the process fairly often.

SCORPION

There are scorpions and pseudo-scorpions, so give anything you are doubtful about a wide berth as you could get a painful sting from a scorpion's tail. Both are worth leaving unmolested because the true scorpion eats cockroaches, and the pseudo-scorpion, which does not sting, eats a variety of other insects.

SKINKS

If you come across a small, flat-scaled lizard hiding under a stone or in your flower pots, welcome it. Skinks live among leaf litter and sprawling vegetation and eat snails, beetles, and unwary moths.

SLUGS

Slugs like to travel on even ground and have difficulty negotiating crumbly compost or a covering of bark. Slugs betray their presence by

Slugs

the slimy trails they leave behind on their nocturnal prowls. They don't like freshly limed ground or wood ash, or the bitterness left behind on the soil by a watering with wormwood tea (see "Herb Teas"). When confronted by a slug, you can kill it by sprinkling salt over it. A kinder death can be offered by putting down saucers of beer for slugs to enjoy before they drown in an alcoholic daze.

SNAILS

Handpicking snails in the garden after a rainy night can be a lengthy but highly satisfying job. Cabbage leaves left on the ground at night will offer snails cover

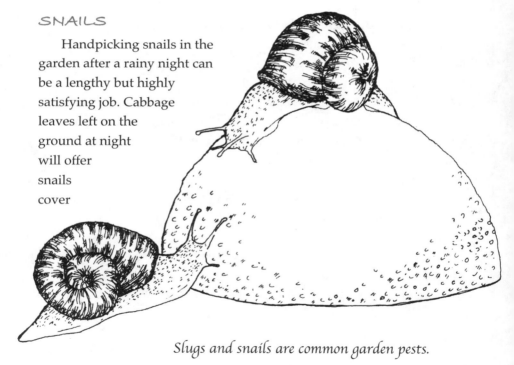

Slugs and snails are common garden pests.

from which they can be collected and destroyed. Birds encouraged to the garden will help keep the snail population down, but probably not low enough. Hand-to-hand combat is the most effective way of getting rid of snails, and citrus skins, left inverted among garden plants, will collect the pests in satisfying numbers for slaughter.

SPIDERS

Spiders eat insects, so they are useful in the garden. Many garden spiders weave circular webs that trap insects. The wolf spider hunts among garden litter, and the bark spider hunts under loose bark. All spiders are valuable predators of insects that are a nuisance to the gardener.

Spider

TACHINID FLIES

If you see a fly that doesn't look quite like an ordinary fly, it is probably the tachinid, which eats cutworms and caterpillars. The tachinid fly should definitely be spared.

THRIPS

Thrips are very small but can make a terrible mess of the leaves of bushes and flowers, eating away the green and leaving silvery disfiguring marks. Thrips are less likely to attack plants growing near pyrethrum.

TOADS

Toads are very useful in the garden, since they come out under cover of night and hunt slugs, cutworms, and many other insects. Unfortunately, toads also eat earthworms, but nobody's perfect.

WASPS

It's better to avoid a wasp than to kill it. Yellow jacket and paper wasps eat grubs, scale insects, and caterpillars. The braconid wasp injects her eggs into aphids (and the eggs and larvae of other insects),

Wasp

and when they hatch, the wasp larvae eat all the fatty tissue and the host dies. There are other intricate ways in which the wasp ensures its survival as a species, and all these methods seem to be at the expense of insects that we can happily do without.

Apart from exercising a useful control over pests, wasps—which are honey-feeders—help pollinate the flower and fruit garden.

I have great faith in a seed.
Convince me that you have a seed
there, and I am prepared to
expect wonders.

~Henry David Thoreau

·····················

chapter 2

A to Z Guide to Companion Plants

A

ALFALFA

The deep-rooted alfalfa plant is an excellent companion to shallow-rooted plants such as grapevines and fruit trees, because they do not compete for soil space. Alfalfa also hinders evaporation and will help keep other plants alive during dry spells.

Keep alfalfa away from any member of the onion family. Also be aware that alfalfa often encourages dandelions, which also have deep roots and will move into the well-prepared soil when the alfalfa dies down.

APPLES

Apple trees grow better in the absence of grass. Grass roots have a breath that shrivels the tender root tips of the apple tree.

Clumps of chives grown around apple trees inhibit the formation of apple scab. If your trees have apple scab, spray with a tea made from chives or horsetail (*Equisetum*) (see "Herb Teas"). When grown around or beneath apple trees, foxgloves impart vitality and increase the trees' (and other plants') strength to resist disease.Growing foxgloves in the vicinity of apple trees also improves the keeping quality of the apples. Furthermore, the sweet-scented wallflower and the apple tree grow better near each other. On the other hand, the potato

Apples are happier when grass is kept away from them.

is much more likely to go down with Phytophtora blight if you plant apple trees near the potato patch.

When stored, apples give off ethylene gas. (This is what gives stored apples their distinctive smell.) Keep carrots and potatoes well away from apples to prevent the carrots from turning bitter and the potatoes from losing their flavor and starting to rot.

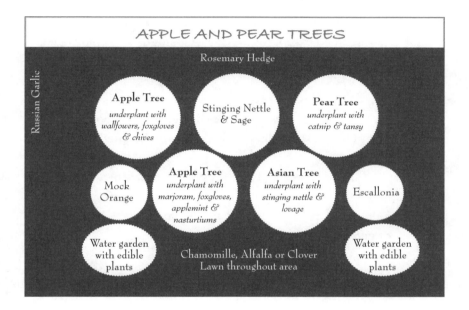

APRICOTS

The roots of the apricot tree and the roots of the tomato plant don't react well to each other, so the plants are best kept well apart. Oats and potatoes should also be planted well away from apricot trees.

Clumps of basil, tansy, or southernwood planted around apricot trees won't entirely stave off fruit flies, but the herbs' scent is likely to make the pests try somewhere else first.

ASPARAGUS

Many gardeners grow asparagus with a mulch of hay and leave the vegetable undisturbed except for picking. Asparagus also enjoys the company of tomatoes and parsley.

ASTERS

Garden pests find the leaves of asters disagreeable in both their smell and their bitter taste. Asters are good flowers to grow for massing and cutting.

Red spider mites may attack asters, but the mites can be held at bay by anise or coriander sprays. To aid an aster plant stricken with powdery mildew, simply spray the plant with an infusion of chives, horsetail, or garlic.

B

BASIL

A garden can't have too much basil. Bush basil, which only grows to 12 inches (30 cm) in height; sweet basil, which grows to three times that height; and ornamental basil, which has purple leaves and doesn't look like either of them—all are the gardener's friend. Bees love basil. Aphids, fruit flies, whiteflies, and house flies hate it.

Basil can be used as an ornamental border around the tomato

patch, making the plants more disease resistant and adding flavor to the fruit. While basil doesn't completely deter fruit flies, it helps, and it looks pretty around your peach and apricot trees.

Whiteflies won't come near basil. Tuck a plant or two near fuchsias to protect them. Pots of basil on windowsills, near open doors, and in outside eating areas will drive the house fly away.

A sprinkling of the powdered leaves adds zest to sliced tomatoes, salads, and soups.

Although they both repel house flies, rue and basil do each other nothing but harm. Rue is very bitter, while basil is sweet.

You can't have too much basil in a garden.

BAY

Bay leaves repel weevils in stored grains (such as wheat, rye, and oats), and in dried legumes (such as beans, peas, and lentils). Scatter bay leaves on the pantry shelves to keep ants away.

Bay trees repel many pests and diseases, and their nearness will benefit more susceptible plants.

BEANS

While the bean family, *Leguminosae*, is very large, we are concerned only with the broad bean, the French bean, and the climbing bean often found in the family garden. Beans can fix nitrogen in the soil. Remember this when choosing a crop to sow in ground where beans have recently grown. Nitrogen encourages leafy growth.

Runner beans can happily occupy the same space, year after year. Family hair clippings, dog and cat combings, sodden newspapers, and dirt emptied from the vacuum cleaner can help runner beans grow well. (They love the mineral and chemical properties in the mixture.)

Dwarf beans, beets, and potatoes planted in alternate rows in their own small patch will help each other to stay healthy and to make a good yield. Broad beans and potatoes planted close to each other will each inhibit the pests that attack the other. All beans grow well near carrots, cucumbers, cabbage, lettuce, peas, parsley, and cauliflower. All beans grow badly near onions, garlic, fennel, or gladioli.

Climbing beans should not be planted near sunflowers as they fight each other for light and space.

Broad beans grow better if planted in alternate rows with spinach, which shades the soil and keeps it damp.

BEETS

Beets grow well with onions, Swiss chard, kohlrabi, lettuce, cabbage, and dwarf beans. Beets do not grow well near tall beans, possibly because the beans don't allow them enough light.

BORAGE

Borage is called the herb of courage. It is a pretty thing with blue flowers and leaves that taste of cucumber. Strawberries grown near borage fight off disease and produce bigger and better-tasting fruit.

BROCCOLI

Broccoli belongs to the cabbage family and has the same characteristics of cabbage, one of which is the ability to stunt the growth of strawberries (see "Cabbage").

Borage

BRUSSELS SPROUTS

Brussels sprouts don't do strawberries any good either. Their own troubles mostly come from attack by mildew and the cutworm.

A light spray of methylated spirits will help Brussels sprouts combat mildew. Narrow collars of tarred paper, or even of plain cardboard, will deter the cutworm. To make the collars, cut the paper or cardboard into 3-inch (7 cm) widths. Cut off in lengths sufficient to make a neat circle around the plant, then staple together. Drop over the plant, sinking an inch (2–3 cm) of the collar into the soil.

C

CABBAGE

Cabbage grows well in the company of beans and beets, celery, mint, thyme, sage, rosemary and dill, onions, and potatoes.

Cabbage does not grow well near strawberries or tomatoes. (The strawberries and tomatoes don't flourish either.) Don't grow cabbage in the same spot two years running, as the plants will be twice as susceptible to clubroot the second year. Don't grow the herb rue anywhere near cabbage plants, as they hate the bitter exhalation from the rue leaves and the excretions given off by the herb's roots.

The cabbage white butterfly looks pretty as it flickers over the garden, but the trick is to dissuade it from settling on your cabbages and laying its eggs on them. This butterfly does not like the scents of sage, rosemary, hyssop, thyme, dill, southernwood, mint, and chamomile, so a border of one or more of these herbs will help keep it away.

Aphids don't like orange-colored nasturtiums, which can look very attractive grown between and around cabbage plants. Aphids *do* like yellow nasturtiums, however. They find the color yellow pleasing and will congregate on the plants. If you grow a few nearby, they will act as a lure and give you the chance to eliminate many of the pests.

Tansy will repel both the cabbage worm and the cutworm. Short sticks of rhubarb buried here and there throughout the cabbage patch will help protect the plants against clubroot.

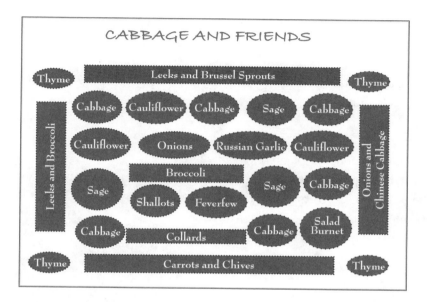

CABBAGE AND FRIENDS

Thyme — Leeks and Brussel Sprouts — Thyme

Cabbage / Cauliflower / Cabbage / Sage / Cabbage

Leeks and Broccoli

Cauliflower / Onions / Russian Garlic / Cauliflower

Onions and Chinese Cabbage

Broccoli

Sage / Shallots / Feverfew / Sage / Cabbage

Cabbage / Collards / Cabbage / Salad Burnet

Thyme — Carrots and Chives — Thyme

Strips of tarred twine or carpet pad stretched between the rows, as well as twists of tinfoil around the cabbage roots, will inhibit the growth of cabbage-fly larvae.

Few insects like bonemeal. A scattering over the plants and between the rows will send them elsewhere. If cabbages show signs of mildew, a light spray with methylated spirits will help.

CAMELLIAS

Camellias like tea leaves. They also like a bit of shade, at least part of the day.

If you use tea bags, slit them and drop them into a container of water. When the color of the water is a pleasant brown, pour the contents around the roots of the trees.

Underplanting camellias with nasturtiums, lavender, or marigolds will deter ants.

CARNATIONS

If carnations are planted in soil where hyacinths have grown, the carnations will be poisoned. Conversely, if hyacinths are planted in soil where carnations have grown, the hyacinths will die.

CARROTS

Carrots grow well with peas, radishes, lettuce, chives, sage, onions, and leeks. Carrots and onions planted in alternate rows are good allies. Carrots drive off the onion fly, while onions drive off the carrot fly.

Carrot roots give off a breath of something that peas appreciate. When you plant them together, keep carrots on the sunny side.

Carrot-fly maggots, which attack

Carrots prefer to grow near peas, radishes, lettuce, chives, sage, onions, and leeks.

the roots of the plant, don't like strong odors. Moth balls crumbled into the soil around the growing carrots, tarred or creosoted string strung between the rows, and pungent herbs (like sage, rosemary, and wormwood) planted nearby will help keep carrot-fly maggots away.

When sowing carrot seed, try to disperse it evenly and thinly. The disturbance of thinning encourages the carrot fly.

For a mixed planting, try sowing leeks and carrots in the same row. Use slightly more carrot seed than leek seed. The carrots will be ready to harvest before the leeks, acting as protection against the carrot fly.

CATMINT

If you have cats, it is fun to grow catmint (nepeta) so you can watch the cats roll ecstatically in it. If you don't have cats, you may still want to grow catmint, as it acts as a deterrent to ants.

CAULIFLOWERS

Cauliflower grows well near celery, which keeps away the white cabbage butterfly. But cauliflower and strawberries should not be planted near each other.

A sprinkling of wood ash around cauliflower plants will protect them against insect attack. To ward off cutworms, fit a cardboard collar around each cauliflower plant, then push the collar a little way into the soil.

CELERY

Celery grows well near tomatoes, dill, beans, leeks, and cabbage. It is particularly happy growing in alternate rows with leeks. Both celery and leeks like compost that has some pig manure in it.

Celery benefits all members of the cabbage family, as the white cabbage butterfly does not like its scent.

CHAMOMILE

Chamomile, or *Anthemis nobilis*, is a pleasure to grow if only for its profusion of golden flowers and elegant ,feathery leaves. Other plants enjoy chamomile's company. Mint becomes tastier when grown near it, and ailing plants tend to revive. Cabbage does all the better for growing near chamomile. Onions also like chamomile—provided it keeps about 3 feet (1 m) away.

Chamomile is often referred to as the "plant doctor." This is because chamomile's nearness encourages other plants to increase their essential oils and therefore to taste and smell more strongly.

At one time an anthemis lawn was popular, not only because insects won't breed in it, but also because it stays green throughout the driest weather and gives off a clean scent when walked on. But chamomile does flower

Chamomile—
"the plant doctor"

continually and can grow quite tall, so it takes a fair amount of work to keep in trim. (A chamomile lawn is likely to be the Treneague strain, which never flowers and never requires cutting.) Do not mix the two strains of chamomile.

If you collect and dry chamomile flowers, you can use them to make chamomile tea by soaking a handful in cold water for a day or two. Any young plant that looks sickly will be helped by a gentle dose of the "medicine."

Old chamomile plants can be grubbed out, chopped up, and added to the compost bin to help to activate the composting process.

CHERVIL

Most herbs are happier grown in company with others. Chervil, which is such a pleasant flavoring for baby carrots, is happiest alongside dill and coriander. It is also a good companion to radishes, making them hotter and crisper.

CHIVES

Chives are almost never attacked by disease or insects. Chives and parsley grow well together. Clumps of chives growing near apple trees will help keep the trees free of apple scab.

Apple trees suffering from scab can be sprayed with chive tea. Make this tea by infusing dried chives in boiling water, letting the water cool, and then using it at half strength.

Chives tea is also a useful spray when gooseberry bushes start to show mildew.

CITRUS

When planting several citrus trees, plant a guava tree nearby. The guava tree will protect the citrus trees from infection. It is said that a few zinc-coated nails gently hammered into a citrus-tree trunk will ensure a good crop.

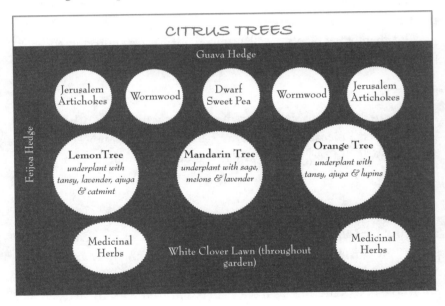

CITRUS TREES

Guava Hedge

Feijoa Hedge

Jerusalem Artichokes

Wormwood

Dwarf Sweet Pea

Wormwood

Jerusalem Artichokes

LemonTree
underplant with tansy, lavender, ajuga & catmint

Mandarin Tree
underplant with sage, melons & lavender

Orange Tree
underplant with tansy, ajuga & lupins

Medicinal Herbs

White Clover Lawn (throughout garden)

Medicinal Herbs

COMFREY

Comfrey is a splendid plant to have in the garden. Nothing can equal the comfort of a poultice of its large, hairy leaves around a sprained ankle. The ancients called it "Knitbone," and they knew what they were talking about.

Comfrey is rich in potassium, nitrogen, and phosphates and so makes a good fertilizer. Soak a handful of comfrey leaves in water for a month and then strain and use as you would any liquid fertilizer. Dump the resulting sludgy mess among your tomatoes or potatoes.

Comfrey also supplies vitamin B12 and calcium, so try it as a refreshing drink made by pouring 3 cups (.75 L) boiling water over 6 washed, chopped leaves. Allow it to brew like ordinary tea and then serve with a slice of lemon and honey to taste.

CORIANDER

Coriander is a tall annual herb that resembles parsley and tends to attract bees. Coriander grows well with dill, chervil, and anise but wilts near fennel. In return, coriander prevents fennel from forming seed.

When grown between rows of carrots and cabbage, the herbs dill, chervil, and coriander will protect the vegetables from predation by pests.

CORN

I love walking to the garden to pick fresh cobs of corn for lunch. In my garden, the corn is usually intermingled with cucumbers, melons, and, of course, string beans and peas to restore the nitrogen corn takes from the soil. On the outer edge is lettuce, corn salad, small peppers, and summer squash. In a no-dig garden, I grow potatoes under the mulch layer, corn on the the mulch layer, and interplant with herbs and lettuce. This blending of plants produces very tasty potatoes. Peanuts grown with corn reduced borers and other pests.

COREOPSIS

If you want a trouble-free flower that provides lovely blooms for cutting, go for the coreopsis. It is heat resistant, grows equally well in damp, dry, sandy, or heavy soils, and seeds easily. Seed scattered in neglected garden spots in autumn will provide a lovely spring and summer show.

COSMOS

Cosmos, like the coreopsis, is unlikely to be troubled by either pests or disease and is just as good-tempered. It will grow in any type of soil and needs no special care except for an occasional stake for support that will be easily hidden in a group planting. This tall, autumn-flowering annual is great for hiding fences.

CUCUMBERS

Cucumbers are friendly plants that get along well with potatoes, beans, celery, lettuce, sweet corn, and savoy cabbage. Cucumbers love to have sunflowers towering over them to provide shade.

Cucumbers

They appreciate the proximity of

radishes, which repel the cucumber beetle.

If cucumber plants are afflicted by eelworm, spray the plants with sugar solution.

To prevent or treat mildew, spray cucumber plants with nettle tea (see "Herb Teas"). The spray will also act as a fertilizer.

D

DANDELIONS

Some people use the shaggy, golden heads of the dandelion to make wine; others shred the strong, bitter leaves to give sharpness to salads; and still others roast the roots, grind them, and use the powder instead of coffee. All such personal experiments have ended in failure for me. But the dandelion is such a vibrant plant, so rich in copper and bursting with therapeutic qualities, that one can only feel guilt in grubbing it up and

*Dandelions—
rich in copper.*

throwing it away.

The dandelion gives off ethylene gas, which induces plants in the vicinity to mature early. Plants spurred on in this way don't usually do much good after maturity.

When the dandelion has grown and produced its first flowers, cut off stems, leaves, and flowers and add them to the compost where they can be used to help the mixture to mature. The root left below ground will push up more growth that can be used in the same way later.

DILL

Dill has existed since time immemorial. It was known both to the ancient Egyptians and the early Norsemen. Its name comes from the old Norse word *dilla,* which means "to soothe." Dill grows well with fennel and coriander and

Dill grows well with fennel and coriander.

is pleasant to have in the garden, if only for the centuries-long chain of fretful children who slept more easily because their wind was settled by a dose of dill water.

Carrots and tomatoes benefit from having dill close by as it lures away pests. But it should be pulled before it flowers, for after that it seems to be of no further benefit to the plants.

Dill attracts bees and repels to the white cabbage moth.

A few sprigs of dill added to cooking cabbage will nullify the smell for which cabbage has such a bad reputation.

F

FENNEL

If you have a dog, you need fennel in the garden. Fennel can be planted in a pot outside the kennel to deter fleas, and it can be used as a flea-fighting spray inside the kennel.   Pick fennel, scrunch it in your hand until the juices flow, and rub the juices into your dog's coat. The dog will like the aniseed flavor, but fleas will hate it.

If you have a dog, you need fennel.

If you plant fennel in the garden, keep it away from beans (all types), tomatoes, kohlrabi, and coriander. Fennel and coriander have a mutually destroying effect.

Never plant wormwood near fennel, as the fennel will die.

FOXGLOVES

Old-fashioned purple foxglove will stimulate the growth of potatoes, tomatoes, and apples when planted near them. It will also protect them from fungal disease. Foxglove, from which the heart medicine Digitalis is made, can give strength and longer life to plants growing near it. Foxglove tea, made by steeping the flowers, leaves, and stems in water, can be added to the water of vase flowers to keep them healthier for longer.

FUCHSIAS

Once you have ferns in the garden, it is unlikely to be long before you find you have too many. Cull the plants, chop the cullings, and dig them in around your fuchsias.

G

GARLIC

A garden cannot afford to be without garlic. However, remember that peas, beans, cabbage, and strawberries don't like garlic anywhere near them.

Clumps of garlic have been planted in rose gardens for a long time.

It is generally accepted that the pungent breath of the garlic helps keep rosebushes free from aphids.

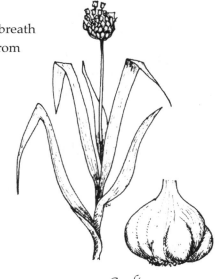

Garlic

When planted beneath apple trees, garlic will help protect them from apple scab. Garlic planted under peach trees will help protect them from leaf curl. And when planted near tomatoes, garlic will help protect the plants from the red spider mite.

Mosquitoes keep away from areas where garlic is growing. Garlic can be grown in pots and shifted around as needed.

Ants, spiders, caterpillars, cabbage worms, and tomato worms can be killed off by a spray made from 4 crushed cloves of garlic soaked in a quart (1 L) of water for several days.

A more potent spray can be made by grinding 2 cloves of garlic and 6 hot red peppers and adding them to water made frothy by 2 tablespoons of soap (not detergent). Use hot water to make the mix, and use your discretion in choosing the temperature at which to spray. Plants can be surprisingly tolerant of the temperature at which sprays are used, but test carefully.

GERANIUMS

Geraniums are showy plants that add color to the garden. If you have a grapevine, spread some geranium cuttings around it and the growing plants will repel the Japanese beetle, which can be such a nuisance to vines. Caterpillars like to eat geraniums, so keep them away by spraying with a mixture of pepper and soapy water.

Geraniums

GLADIOLI

Keep them well away from strawberries, peas, and beans. The flower bed tends to be a good place for them as they seem to grow happily alongside other bulbs, such as iris.

GRAPEVINES

The word goes that grapevines grow better near mulberry trees, where they can twine their way among the branches. I've never had the nerve to do this, having too much trouble trying to collect the mulberries from the tall, madly spreading tree to want to have to clamber after inaccessible grapes. The tip could be worthwhile, but if your nerve fails too, plant hyssop and basil near the vines instead.

H

HERBS

Herbs are happiest when grown in the company of other herbs. So for culinary use, it is good to have a mixed herb patch.

When planting herbs as protection, it follows that one or two species planted together will do a better job.

Annual herbs shouldn't be planted in the same spot two years in succession, since they take too much from the soil in the first year to sustain a crop in the second.

Mix dried herbs with seed when planting to help keep away birds, mice, and slugs.

HORSERADISH

A plant or two of horseradish will protect fruit trees and potatoes against fungus. A plant at each end of the potato plot will be enough, and an occasional one will do good in the orchard. When you think of how too much horseradish sauce can bring tears to the eyes, it is easy to understand why pests steer clear. Young horseradish leaves made into a tea according the recipe under "Herb Teas" is useful as a spray when fruit trees show signs of moniliophthora pod rot.

HORSETAIL

The weed *equisetum* has long been used by herbalists for the

treatment of kidney complaints and is
versatile enough to have been used as
a brass polish. It is a rich source of
silica and when made into a spray is
useful against mildew and fungus.
Used lightly over young plants,
this spray will prevent them from
"damping off." You can buy the dried
herb in health food shops.

To make an herb "tea," boil a
tablespoonful of the dried herb in 2 quarts
(2 L) of water for 20 minutes. Let the
liquid stand covered for 2 days,
and then strain and use.

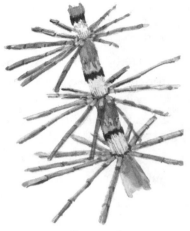

Horsetail

HYSSOP

Bees love the minty-flavored leaves and
blue flowers of hyssop, but radishes won't
grow well in its vicinity.

Grapevines do better with hyssop
growing near them. And a border of hyssop
around the cabbage bed will lure the
cabbage moth away from the cabbages.

When a plant has bacterial disease, spray
it with tea made from hyssop leaves.

Hyssop

K

KOHLRABI

This vegetable, a relative of the cabbage and the turnip, is not grown as often as it deserves, largely because people complain that it is "woody." But kohlrabi only grows woody with age and should be eaten when small. It is good grown near beets and onions, but must be kept away from tomatoes, which it harms, and beans, which harm it.

L

LARKSPUR

The larkspur is not fond of heat, but if you can grow it, the blue, pink, and rose-colored blooms look attractive in the garden and make excellent cut flowers. An added bonus is that larkspur leaves are poisonous to most insect pests, including aphids and thrips.

LAVENDER

Lavender attracts bees and is generally beneficial to the garden. Lavender is said to keep away caterpillars, mice, ticks, and rabbits.

Lavender attracts bees.

LEEKS

Leeks grown in alternate rows with carrots do well, as the plants mutually protect each other.

Leeks and celery, grown in alternate rows in ground enriched with pig- or goat-manure compost, will both benefit from the potassium supplied. Leeks will also benefit from being planted near onions or celeriac. Poor companions for leeks include broad beans and broccoli.

LEGUMES

Almost all plants in the garden are helped by association with the family *Leguminosae*, which, among others, includes the bean and the pea. Legumes take nitrogen from the air and pass it to their roots, which develop nodules that release nitrogen into the soil. Nitrogen produces leafy growth so it is easy to understand why the onion family and the legume family are at cross purposes. But the potato thrives on the nitrogen supplied by pea roots. As a rule of thumb, it is simplest to accept that all members of the onion family are at war with all members of the *Leguminosae* family, and that peas and beans come off worse in the battle. Fruit trees and grapevines appreciate nitrogen in the soil, so they can be planted with advantage where peas and/or beans have been growing.

LEMON BALM

This is a wonderful herb, though regrettably untidy. It is useful for making a fresh, clean herb tea for drinking in hot weather, for using (fresh or dried) in cooking, and for bringing bees into the garden. For this reason, lemon balm is beneficial planted near orchards, as the bees will help pollinate the fruit trees. It will also improve yield for both cucumbers and tomato vines. Lemon balm can be used as a border edging, providing it is clearly established who is boss.

LETTUCE

Lettuce can be a tricky thing to grow. The lettuce plant has a root system that wants what it wants when it wants it, or it can turn cantankerous.

Lettuce enjoys the company of carrots, onions, strawberries, and beets.

Lettuce requires a steady supply of both moisture and nutriment and, if allowed to wilt when half grown, will turn to seed. You have to keep your eye on lettuce.

Lettuce enjoys the company of carrots, onions, strawberries, and beets. Providing water requirements are observed, a plot sown with lettuce, cabbage, and beets will be relatively trouble free.

When planted in alternate rows with radish, lettuce can thrive and, at the same time, protect the radish against the flea beetle.

Wood ash scattered between the rows helps protect lettuce from insect depredations. Best of all, lettuce appreciates the company of the French marigold or the African marigold—the Tagetes species. These small and showy plants should never be confined to the flower garden as they are frontline battlers against insects, which hate the scent of marigold's foliage and blossoms. Lettuce and French marigolds make as natural a marriage as ham and eggs.

LILY OF THE VALLEY

The scent of the lily of the valley is such a delicious harbinger of spring that everyone tries to grow the plant. However, many fail because they do not provide the hard winter conditions the plant needs. If you can offer a cold winter, semi-shade, a soil rich in humus, and woodland conditions, plant the "pips" in early winter and top-dress them with leaf mold or peat. The lily of the valley will flower with the narcissus but don't ever put the cut flowers together in a vase because both of them will wilt.

M

MANGOES

Mangoes attract fruit flies and aphids. To deter fruit flies, plant tansy, basil, and southernwood around the mango tree. Marigolds planted nearby will help keep away the aphids.

Avoid bruising or twisting the fruit stems, as it can cause stem rot.

Starting at the bottom of the tree trunk, hammer in a galvanized iron nail at about 3-foot (1-m) intervals and continue until the branches start to spread. This is said to ensure a bumper crop of fruit.

MARIGOLDS

I asked a friend what he understood by the term "companion planting." He said, "Marigolds with everything."

I grew up with marigolds. My grandmother used to scatter the dried petals on her soups, and she kept calendula ointment at the ready for our grazes and wounds. Her garden burned with the color of marigolds. Many people love the color orange, but just as many hate it. Fortunately for the latter, the *Compositae* family is a large one and includes flowers of

"Marigolds with everything."

Marjoram positively affects plants growing near it.

soft cream, lemon, and apricot. But all marigolds have a strong, unpleasant odor, especially the smaller varieties: the French and African marigolds of the "Tagetes" variety.

Marigold roots give off a substance that drives away the nematode or eelworm. Therefore, it is beneficial to plants marigolds near potatoes, tomatoes, and roses. The Mexican beetle forsakes bean rows that have marigolds growing among them.

A clump of marigolds is useful in every flower bed, and an edging in the vegetable garden helps protect the veggies. I once saw a very pretty border of French marigolds backed by the soft blue of ageratum, which cooled their color and gave them charm.

Marigolds make good cut flowers and are easy to grow. And dogs won't urinate on pots that contain marigold.

MARJORAM

There are two varieties of marjoram: the "sweet," which is an annual, and the "pot," which is a perennial. Both varieties have a good effect on any plants growing near them, and both repel insects. Marjoram attracts bees, however, which will help pollinate your garden. Marjoram and bell peppers are said to be good companions. Marjoram is also a beneficial companion to sage.

Marjoram, a medicinal herb, contains a volatile oil that, when distilled, can be used as a liniment.

MIGNONETTE

With its strange green and brown flowers, this old-fashioned plant has a subtly delightful fragrance. It will benefit rosebushes when used as a ground cover for the beds. Oddly, when placed in a vase with other flowers, mignonette will kill them.

MINT

Mint is a must for every garden. A purchased mint sauce is a pale shadow of a freshly made mint sauce.

Mint grows better in some shade. Planted near the cabbage patch, mint will repel the cabbage white butterfly. Caterpillars and the black flea beetle don't like mint either. Mint is also a good companion for tomatoes; it repels aphids and white flies. Mint will attract beneficial insects, such as hoverflies and wasps.

Fresh or dried mint in the pantry will keep ants away; sachets of dried mint smell nice in the wardrobe and will repel the clothes moth.

Never plant mint near parsley. They don't like each other.

MULBERRIES

Birds love mulberries, and there are always enough on a tree to spare some. Once attracted to the garden, birds do good work by eating all manner of insects, although other fruit may need protection against them.

The mulberry is good for vines that grow happily near them and use them as a means "to climb and spread."

N

NASTURTIUMS

Nasturtiums are irritatingly rampant growers, but before you succumb to the impulse to rip them out, consider the good they do.

Orange-colored nasturtiums repel aphids. If you allow them to grow under and even to twine up apple trees, they will control the spread of the woolly aphid.

Nasturtiums grown in the greenhouse will protect more precious plants against

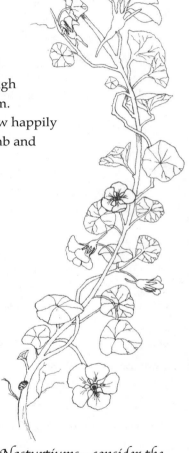

Nasturtiums—consider the good they do.

white fly.

Nasturtiums secrete a mustard oil that insects find attractive, so insects will seek out nasturtiums in preference to cabbage, cauliflower, broccoli, Brussels sprouts, kohlrabi, and turnips growing nearby. Therefore, it makes good sense to let nasturtiums wander between these crops to act, not only as ground cover to keep the soil moist, but as a decoy for insects and as a flavor-improving agent for your crops.

Nasturtiums are particularly good for giving radishes a good, hot taste, and for keeping away cucumber beetles.

NETTLES

Nettles are weeds, and many tidy gardeners make haste to get rid of them. But the nettle is too rich in iron and nitrogen to be destroyed. The nettle excretes silica, formic acid, nitrogen, iron, and protein, and therefore gives strength and flavor to any crop growing nearby. Nettles also protect other plants from aphids, black fly, and mildew.

If you find nettles growing in the potato patch or near your horseradish plants, be grateful. The weeds are particularly good for them both.

As described under "Herb Teas," a tea made from nettles is useful both as a spray against aphids and as a tonic for your plants. The slush left should be added to the compost, where it will help it to decompose more readily.

Another way of using nettles is to leave them in rainwater for three weeks to let them ferment. The resulting liquid makes a good fertilizer.

Any lonely nettle should be transplanted to the tomato area. The more nettles growing there, the better chance the tomatoes won't mold.

If you just have to pull out nettles, don't burn them. Throw them in the compost bin or chop them and dig them into the soil.

O

OAK

Oak trees are known for aiding and protecting the plants and trees surrounding them, especially citrus and chestnut trees. Make a mulch of oak leaves to control cutworms, slugs, snails, and some maggots.

ONIONS

Onions can suffer badly from attack by thrips, and it's unlikely that you'll have enough hoverflies around to protect your crop, so make it part of a mixed planting. Onions grow well in alternate rows with carrots, which protect them against the onion fly, and with beets, Swiss chard, and lettuce. A scattering of wood ash between the rows will give onions added protection.

Onions planted near apple trees will ward off apple scab and minced onion peelings dug into the rose bed will help to keep the roses free of bugs.

To make a spray that is useful against the red spider mite and the aphid (particularly the rose aphid), chop onions (with skins on) to a milky consistency in the food blender, then dilute the resultant liquid by half.

OREGANO

Oregano is an herb that can be substituted for marjoram. Beetles and the white cabbage butterfly won't come near oregano, so it's good to grow among cabbage.

P

PARSLEY

Parsley is said to only grow well in a garden where the woman is the boss, when actually it grows well when anyone has the sense to give it some shade and keep it away from mint. A few parsley plants are never enough, and a thick border is a joy. It takes a great deal of parsley to keep up with family demand for use in cooking, as a garnish, as a tea, or as an astringent for the complexion and a conditioner for the hair.

Parsley—give it some shade and keep it away from mint.

Bees love parsley. Aphids hate it, so it's good to grow near tomatoes, asparagus, and roses. Parsley is said to improve the taste of fruits and vegetables and to increase the scent of roses.

Parsley and chives make good companions.

PARSNIPS

Parsnips' dislikes are easy to remember: carrot, celery, caraway. Parsnips like peas, potatoes, and pepper, and they won't fall out with beans, radishes, or garlic.

The parsnip flower attracts predator wasps and hoverflies, which help keep away the codling moth. Planting parsnips with onions will help prevent the carrot root fly maggot from attacking the parsnips.

PEACHES

The eternal vigilance needed to protect stone fruits can put off even the most patient gardener. But tansy and garlic make a good first line of defense. Tansy repels insects, including the peach-tip moth and the fruit fly.

Mothballs hung among the branches of a peach tree can protect from curly leaf. If your tree does get curly leaf, try spraying it with a

Pears

mixture of nettle and equisetum tea, or one of them if you don't have access to both. If you can make enough to soak the soil around the trees too, so much the better.

PEARS

Grass roots give off an excretion that stops pear-tree roots from growing, so it's best to have an area of grass-free ground around the tree. Surround pear trees with plenty of bee-attracting flowering plants to ensure adequate pollination. Pear trees also prefer a nitrogen-rich soil—chicken or other animal manure should do the trick.

PEAS

Peas grow well with most vegetables but heartily dislike being near onions, shallots, and garlic. Peas should not be grown in the same place two years in succession because they will have robbed the ground of the feed they require.

Two rows of peas to one of potatoes is beneficial to both vegetables. In addition, low-growing plants such as radish, carrot, and turnip are good to grow with peas. But make sure the carrots have the sunny side of the rows.

Tall plants (such as beans and sweet corn) and spreading plants (such as cucumbers) do no harm to peas, but it is well to provide sufficient room for them all to grow without too much encroachment on each other.

Wood ash sprinkled between the rows will protect peas.

PENNYROYAL

Pennyroyal is a good herb to grow where ants are troublesome. It grows well in damp, shady spots. Pennyroyal is a helpful companion plant for broccoli, Brussels sprouts, and cabbage, as it helps keep away cabbage maggots and other burrowing insects.

POTATOES

Potatoes grow well with peas, beans, cabbage, and sweet corn. Potatoes do not grow well near apple trees, cherry trees, cucumbers, pumpkins, sunflowers, tomatoes, and raspberry canes, all of which make potatoes susceptible to blight. I haven't heard whether the same goes for loganberries or the cultivated blackberry, but since they are such close relations to the raspberry, it might be as well not to take the chance with them either.

Potatoes and sunflowers stunt each other's growth—a fairly obvious situation, since both are strong growing plants and will compete with each other for nutrients. Potatoes should also be kept away from tomatoes, as exudation from the potato plants' roots will prevent the tomatoes from growing well.

Broad beans and potatoes are good to grow together, two rows of beans to one of potatoes. Green beans grown in alternate rows with potatoes will help keep the Colorado beetle away. You can also lure the Colorado beetle away by planting eggplant near your potatoes. Even if you don't like eggplant, it is useful as a lure because beetles prefer it to the potato and will congregate on the plants, where you can dispose of them. Marigolds are said to repel both the Colorado beetle and the eelworm.

Nasturtiums allowed to wander among the potato plants, plus a few horseradish plants and nettles left to grow, will help protect your potato crop.

What exactly the pumpkin and the potato have against each other is not clear, but their animosity is strong and mutual.

Potato beetles love bran. A goodly supply sprinkled between the rows will offer an alternative food supply.

PRIMULAS

If you want your primulas (primroses) to be safe from the pecking of birds, just plant them near the lavender hedge.

PUMPKINS (See also "Squash")

Pumpkins and sweet corn grow well together because the pumpkin provides ground cover. This is particularly effective during a hot, dry summer when the pumpkin keeps the soil cool and conserves water, which helps the corn. Pumpkins do not grow well near potatoes.

PYRETHRUM

Pyrethrum is a pretty little plant that looks nice anywhere. The plant is of particular value near strawberries, as it helps keep pests away.

The dust made from pyrethrum is a safe insecticide for the garden, except for the fact that it kills bees. If you use it in the evening when the bees have retired for the night, you need have no worries.

R

RADISHES

Radishes grow well with lettuce, which controls the flea beetle that attacks the radish. Radishes also grow well near chervil.

Radishes grow badly near the herb hyssop. Nasturtiums, which secrete a mustard oil, give radishes a sharper flavor if grown nearby.

RASPBERRIES

Raspberries do not grow well with blackberries, loganberries, or boysenberries. And raspberries grown near potatoes make the potatoes more susceptible to blight.

Turnips and yarrow tend to be good companions to raspberries, as they keep harlequin beetles away. Garlic, tansy, wormwood, and lavender are also beneficial.

Rhubarb

Raspberries are susceptible to mold, so be sure to pick them right after a heavy rainfall. Then spray the unripened fruit with chamomile. Use a straw mulch around raspberries—it has been shown to produce a higher yield.

RHUBARB

If rhubarb starts flowering, the plants are either short of water or food.

Keep the dock weed away from rhubarb plants, as the weed encourages the presence of the rhubarb curculio, a yellow snout beetle that bores into the stems and leaves.

Short sticks of rhubarb dug in around cabbage will help to protect them against clubroot.

Rhubarb leaves are strong in oxalic acid, so while they may be good for cleaning aluminum, they should not be eaten. They can, however, be used to make a spray to use against aphids. Chop a good, solid mass of rhubarb leaves, then simmer them in water for half an hour. Dilute the liquid to about one-third strength as a spray. Do not, however, store the liquid. Never cook rhubarb in an aluminum saucepan—it's dangerous.

ROSEMARY

The name rosemary comes from the Latin *ros marinus,* which means "dew of the sea." But for the life of me I can't see how this shrubby, aromatic plant earned the name. Certainly it grows well near the sea, but it is also found in the Sahara Desert.

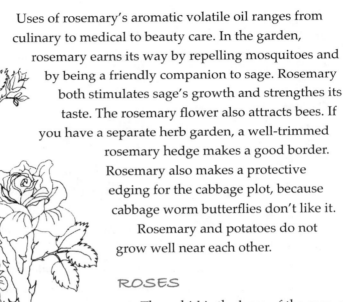

Uses of rosemary's aromatic volatile oil ranges from culinary to medical to beauty care. In the garden, rosemary earns its way by repelling mosquitoes and by being a friendly companion to sage. Rosemary both stimulates sage's growth and strengthes its taste. The rosemary flower also attracts bees. If you have a separate herb garden, a well-trimmed rosemary hedge makes a good border. Rosemary also makes a protective edging for the cabbage plot, because cabbage worm butterflies don't like it. Rosemary and potatoes do not grow well near each other.

ROSES

The aphid is the bane of the rose grower. When planting a new rosebush, place a clove of garlic next to the roots. The roots of the rose will take up the exudation from the garlic and become less attractive to the green fly. Parsley will also help keep the green fly away from roses.

Instead of throwing away your banana skins, tuck them in the soil

Parsley, onion, and garlic make roses smell sweeter.

around your rosebushes. They will provide silica, calcium, sulfur phosphate, and sodium, on which the rosebushes will thrive.

It's unlikely that you'll want to plant onions among your roses, but garlic looks nice. However, onion skins can be chopped and dug into the soil around rosebushes. Both garlic and onions make roses smell even sweeter.

Mignonette looks pleasant as a ground cover beneath rosebushes, and the roses appreciate its presence.

A wide piece of plastic piping sunk about three feet (1 m) deep into the ground by the side of a rosebush is helpful. This simple funnel ensures that water gets to the roots where it is needed and is not just dissipated a few inches below ground.

RUE

Rue is a dainty plant with feathery leaves and golden flowers. No insects will go near rue, and slugs give it a wide berth. This "herb of grace" was once used in exorcism by the Roman Catholic Church. Rue grows easily from seed, enjoys full sun, and is useful as an edging hedge, less than three feet (1 m) high. Keep rue away from sage and basil, as it poisons both of them.

S

SAGE

Sage takes its name from the Latin *salvare*, which means "to heal." Sage is one of the most popular herbs, both for its culinary use and for its attractive appearance. The blue gray leaves and blue flowers blend well with other plants, provided the sage is not allowed to straggle.

Sage protects carrots against the carrot fly, and cabbages against the cabbage moth. Cabbages are more tender when grown near sage. Dried sage sprinkled around plants will protect them from lice and mildew.

When sage is grown near cucumbers, it tends to make the cucumbers take on a bitter taste.

Sage

SALAD BURNET

The leaves of this cooling herb make a great addition to salads or as a sandwich garnish. When growing salad burnet for culinary use, pinch off the flowers as soon as they appear so the outer leaves don't become so bitter.

With its elegant fern-like foliage, this herb makes a nice border for an herb bed or flower bed. Salad burnet is a beneficial companion to mint and thyme.

SANTOLINA

Roses like santolina. The shrub grows to about 24 inches (60 cm) high, and if the silver gray foliage is kept trimmed, it can make a nicely domed little bush. Clipping santolina down in late spring or summer will ensure bushy, aromatic growth. Left untrimmed, santolina will be covered by a mass of yellow button flowers that light up the border.

Santolina deters pests, especially cabbage moths.

SAVORY

Winter savory is a perennial, while summer savory is an annual. Savory is useful, planted between rows of beans, where its peppery leaves inhibit the bean beetle. Onions appreciate savory too. Because bees love savory, it is beneficial to grow it near hives.

SOUTHERNWOOD

Nicknamed "lad's love" or "old man," southernwood has been used over the centuries to treat worms in children, female menstrual difficulties, and baldness in men, and to keep moths out of carpets. Its silver gray leaves are bitter to the taste and it has a sharp scent.

A hedge of southernwood will grow to less than three feet (1 m) in height, and if kept trimmed will look decorative while repelling the fruit fly and the mosquito.

Planting southernwood with fruit trees will protect the trees from moths and fruit flies, and planting it with roses will protect them from aphids. Planting southernwood with cabbage will protect it from the cabbage white butterfly. And finally, planting southernwood with carrots will protect them from the carrot root fly.

SOYBEANS

Soybeans are an overall benefit to the garden. They prepare the soil for other plants by fixing nitrogen into the soil with their roots, and by nourishing and reconditioning poor soil. Soybeans are said to ward off corn borers, corn ear worms, and Japanese beetles in corn crops. Soybeans also attract certain beneficial predatory wasps.

SPINACH

Spinach needs cool conditions and may run to seed in hot weather. It likes to grow near strawberries. Although it is rich in iron, calcium, and vitamins A and C, it is also high in oxalic acid, so don't be like Popeye and live on it. Enjoy it served with lemon and butter or pureed with a sprinkling of nutmeg, fairly often but not frequently.

Spinach is a good companion plant for cabbages, onion, peas, and celery. But keep spinach away from grapevines and hyssop.

SQUASH

The term *squash* is used herein to refer to zucchinis, pumpkins, chayote, cucumber, and melons. They are all gross feeders, and slugs just love

Squash

them. Don't leave their pollination to bees and other insects; take a personal hand. The female flower, unlike the male flower, has a swelling behind it. You can use a cotton swab or fine paintbrush to transfer the pollen from the male flower to the female flower, but if they are close enough together, you can jam the open flowers together and give them a shake to transfer the pollen.

All varieties of squash are tastiest when small, since the larger fruit are mostly water. One delicious variety is spaghetti squash. The bright yellow fruits are about 8 inches (20 cm) in length. When the flesh is boiled, it looks like spaghetti but is lower on the glycemic index and contains more fiber and vitamins.

STRAWBERRIES

Strawberries dislike being near cabbage, cauliflower, Brussels sprouts, broccoli, and gladioli. They need well-drained soil and regular feeding and watering. Strawberries enjoy growing near borage, lettuce, spinach, and sage.

Strawberries

A mulch of crushed pine needles or pinecones will give strawberries added flavor. A mulch of any sort will keep weeds down and prevent moisture loss. Try grass clippings, compost, sawdust, leaf mold, or wood shavings.

An edging of pyrethrum around the strawberry bed will keep many pests away. And a low cage of wire mesh over the bed will protect the fruit from the birds.

SUNFLOWERS

The sunflower makes a spectacular display and attracts bees to the garden. Squash and cucumber grow well in the shade of the tall plants. But sunflowers should be kept well away from potatoes as they stunt each other's growth.

Sunflowers improve soil by secreting a substance that inhibits the growth of nearby weeds. They do require, however, a compost-rich soil.

Sunflowers help to attract pest-controlling birds, bees, and bugs, including hoverflies, lacewings, and predatory wasps.

SWEET CORN

Sweet corn is benefitted when grown near broad beans, potatoes, melons, cucumber, and squash. Sweet corn, grown near tomatoes, will lure away the pest heliothis.

Sweet corn takes a great deal of nitrogen from the soil, so it is good to replace it with peas and beans as a following crop.

Corn earworm is a pest that burrows itself in between the corn kernels. As sprays do not affect the earworm, it is best to encourage birds, which will feed on the earworm. You may also try deterring earworms with a companion crop of sunflowers.

SWISS CHARD

Onions and beets are Swiss chard's favorite companions; it is also said to grow well near lavender. Swiss chard likes a nitrogen-rich soil, so add plenty of chicken manure to its soil. Prone to fungal disease, Swiss chard should be treated with a chamomile spray.

T

TANSY

You may know tansy as "bachelor's buttons," a name that well describes the little yellow flowers that grow in a cluster at the top of the stems. With its pleasant, feathery leaves and bright color, it is one of the most cheerful and useful plants in the garden.

Tansy is a strong insect repellent. Insects hate its bitter taste and strong odor. Tansy's leaves and stems are poisonous to humans and animals, but it's doubtful if either would be willing to eat them anyway. I rub the crushed leaves into my dog's coat to help protect her from fleas.

Tansy is good to plant near cabbages, roses, raspberries, and grapes, among other plants. Tansy concentrates potassium in the soil and so benefits nearby growth.

Plant tansy wherever you need protection against cutworms, cabbage worms, ants, flies, mosquitoes, and fruit moths. Tansy is particularly good beneath peach trees, as it helps them stay healthy. It also wards off flying insects and keeps borers away.

Tansy was one of the "strewing herbs" used in the old days to prevent insects from infesting the straw scattered on dirt floors. Today tansy can be used in the food cupboard to discourage ants, and in the clothes cupboard to drive out moths, or better still, to prevent them from settling in at all.

Chopped-up tansy makes a good activator for the compost heap.

TARRAGON

An aromatic herb, tarragon is helpful to most other plants, giving weak plants an extra boost. Tarragon seems to be especially beneficial to eggplants and bell peppers.

THISTLE

Thistles are a nice addition to the compost heap because they are rich in potassium and silica. But thistles can be harmful to grain crops because they are greedy feeders, so make sure your thistles don't go to seed.

THYME

There are many varieties of thyme—lemon, caraway, turkey, variegated, etc. All are pleasant to have in the garden if only for the fact that they attract bees.

When grown near plants in the cabbage family, thyme will help deter the cabbage root fly. Dried thyme sprinkled around the rows will help too. All plants growing near thyme are invigorated by it.

Thyme makes a pleasant small shrub. It can also be grown in pots for use in salads and to flavor tomatoes. The dried leaves are useful in cooking.

Thyme contains thymol, a powerful disinfectant. Thyme was used in incense burners to purify sickrooms. Its oil is said to be more than ten times stronger as a disinfectant than carbolic acid.

TOMATOES

Tomatoes grow well near asparagus, celery, parsley, basil, carrots, and chives. But they do not enjoy the company of rosemary, potatoes, kohlrabi, and fennel.

Some experts advise

Tomatoes and basil—the perfect pair.

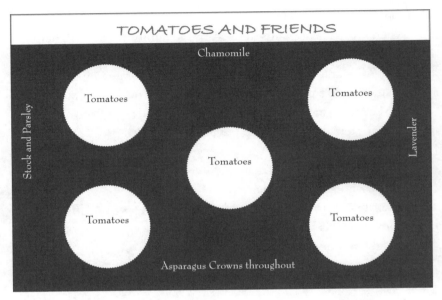

TOMATOES AND FRIENDS

Chamomile

Tomatoes

Tomatoes

Stock and Parsley

Tomatoes

Lavender

Tomatoes

Tomatoes

Asparagus Crowns throughout

keeping tomatoes away from all members of the cabbage family; others advise growing them together because tomatoes ward off the cabbage white butterfly. Since there is doubt, it seems better to me to rely on thyme, mint, hyssop, rosemary, southernwood, and sage to look after the cabbage family, and keep tomatoes away in case they should suffer from being gallant.

Tomatoes can be protected against the cutworm by sowing iron nails in the soil around them, from nematodes by growing French marigolds nearby, and from mold by giving them the company of nettles.

Grown near gooseberry bushes, tomatoes help protect the bushes against insect attack. But tomatoes should not be grown near apricot trees, as a substance given off by tomato-plant roots can harm the trees.

Tomato leaves reportedly contain a substance more active than nicotine. Soak a handful of tomato leaves in water for a day, then spray the water on fruit trees and rosebushes to fight aphids. It also deters caterpillars. If virus attacks your tomato plants, spray them with milk.

TULIPS

If you plant summer-blooming shrubs and ferns next to tulips, the shrubs will hide the dying tulips as summer progresses. (It is important to keep the dying tulips in the soil as they become food for the following year's flowers.)

Be careful not to let the soil around tulips get too wet, as tulips bulbs have a tendency to rot. Mice like to nibble on the tulip bulbs. To keep mice away from tulips, sink a wire cage into the soil around the bulbs, or plant mice-repelling herbs, such as spearmint. Tulips also inhibit the growth of wheat, so plant the bulbs away from this grain.

TURNIPS

Turnips grow well with peas and appreciate the protection of wood ash sprinkled around them. As farmers say, "If all else fails, grow turnips." Turnips are light feeders and nicest if harvested before fully mature. It is best to grow turnips in direct sunlight.

Control aphids and turnip sawflies with a pyrethrum spray.

V

VALERIAN

Valerian is useful in compost as it is rich in phosphorus. It also attracts earthworms, which help aerate soil. These two qualities make it an excellent companion plant. A tea spray made from valerian is said to promote healthy growth in sickly plants.

W

WALLFLOWERS

The wallflower, a fragrant perennial, is best treated as an annual in a cool climate. Wallflowers like full sun and a soil previously dressed with lime and old manure. To keep cut wallflowers alive longer, split the ends of the stem and crush lightly, dip into boiling water for a few seconds, and then let the stems rest in deep water for half an hour.

Wallflowers are a good companion for apple trees.

Wallflowers—good companions for apple trees.

WORMWOOD

An aromatic plant with gray green silvery leaves and small yellow flowers, wormwood keeps moths as a distance. Wormwood should be kept to itself because its toxic root excretions harm plants growing nearby. Even other aromatic plants such as sage and fennel cannot cope with wormwood. However, it is very helpful to grow wormwood in the vicinity of fruit trees as a guard against leaf-eating caterpillars, aphids, and moths.

Wormwood discourages fleas, mosquitoes, slugs, mice, and the cabbage worm butterfly. Wormwood tea poured on the ground will deter slugs or mice.

If you injure yourself while working in the garden and don't have any disinfectant on hand, place a few wormwood leaves in boiling water for a short time, then cool the leaves and use them as a poultice on the wound.

After washing your dog, drench him or her with wormwood tea (see "Herb Teas") to help get rid of fleas.

Y

YARROW

Once regarded as a weed, yarrow is now a garden favorite. It is a pleasant plant with feathery leaves and flowers of white, yellow, red, and pink. Dwarf yarrow and tall yarrow are useful for blending among other plants, since they increase the vitality of their neighbors.

If you find your soil is deficient in copper, you need yarrow as a fertilizer. Yarrow is valuable when added to compost, and yarrow tea can be used as a liquid medicine (see "Herb Teas"). Yarrow tea is also said to be good for rheumatism, and the young leaves, when chewed, give temporary relief from toothache.

Yarrow is a good companion plant for vegetables, especially cucumbers and corn. It also seems to benefit other herbs, increasing their essential oil content and aroma.

Yarrow attracts beneficial insects, such as ladybugs and predatory wasps.

Yarrow

It also seems to have a repelling effect on certain unwanted pests.

Z

ZUCCHINI

What could look nicer than the bold colors of the nasturtium against the deep green of zucchini leaves? In addition to creating a pleasant picture, nasturtiums protect zucchini from aphids.

Zucchini is a beneficial companion to beans, mint, radishes, and sweet corn. It germinates quickly and grows thickly, so it helps choke out weeds.

Zucchini is susceptible to mold and fungal diseases, so be sure to plant zucchini in a well-drained, airy location in your garden.

The fair-weather gardener,
who will do nothing except
when the wind and weather and
everything else are favorable, is
never master of his craft.
~Henry Ellacombe

....

chapter 5

Good Companions/
Bad Companions

Good Companions

Allliums*	beet, tomato,lettuce, carrots, brassicas
Apples	Chives, horsetail (*Equisetum*), foxgloves, wallflowers, nasturtiums
Apricots	Basil, tansy, southernwood
Artichoke	Potatoes, broad beans
Asparagus	Tomatoes, parsley, basil
Basil	Tomatoes, asparagus, parsley, apricots

Beans	Carrots, cucumbers, cabbage, lettuce, peas, parsley, cauliflower, spinach
Beans, dwarf	Beets, potatoes
Beets	Onions, Swiss chard, kohlrabi, lettuce, cabbage, dwarf beans
Borage	Strawberries
Brassicas	Potatoes, celery, beets, alliums, tomatoes
Cabbages	Beans, beets, celery, mint, thyme, sage, rosemary, dill, potatoes, chamomile, oregano
Carrots	Peas, radishes, lettuce, chives, sage, onions, leeks
Cauliflowers	Celery, beans
Celery	Tomatoes, dill, beans, leeks, cabbage, cauliflowers
Chamomile	Mint, cabbage
Chervil	Dill, coriander
Chives	Parsley, apples, carrots
Citrus	Guava
Coriander	Dill, chervil, anise, cabbage, carrots

Corn	Potatoes, peas, beans, cucurbits
Cucumbers	Potatoes, beans, celery, lettuce, sweet corn, savoy cabbage, sunflowers, radishes
Dill	Carrots, tomatoes
Eggplant	Carrots, radish, cucurbits, alliums, tomatoes
Foxgloves	Tomatoes, potatoes, apples
Horseradish	Fruit trees, potatoes
Hyssop	Grapevines, cabbage
Kohlrabi	Beets, onions
Garlic	Roses, apples, peaches
Geraniums	Grapevines
Grapevines	Geraniums, mulberries, hyssop, basil, peas, beans
Guava	Citrus
Leeks	Carrots, celery
Lettuce	Carrots, onions, strawberries, beets, cabbage, radishes, marigolds

Marigolds	Lettuce, potatoes, tomatoes, roses, beans
Mint	Cabbage
Nasturtiums	Apples, cabbage, cauliflowers, broccoli, Brussels sprouts, kohlrabi, turnips, radishes, cucumbers, zucchini
Onions	Carrots, beets, Swiss chard, lettuce
Oregano	Cabbage
Parsley	Tomatoes, asparagus, roses, chives
Parsnips	Peas, potatoes, peppers, beans, radishes, garlic
Peaches	Tansy, garlic
Peas	Potatoes, radishes, carrots, turnips
Potatoes	Peas, beans, cabbage, sweet corn, broad beans, nasturtiums, marigolds
Pumpkins	Sweet corn
Radishes	Lettuces, peas, chervil, nasturtiums
Roses	Garlic, parsley, onions, mignonette
Sage	Carrots, cabbage

Savory	Beans, onions
Spinach	Strawberries
Strawberries	Borage, lettuce, spinach, sage
Sunflowers	Squash, cucumber
Sweet corn	Broad beans, potatoes, melons, tomatoes, cucumbers, squash
Swiss chard	Onions, beets, lavender
Tansy	Cabbage, roses, raspberries, grapes, peaches
Thyme	Cabbage family
Tomatoes	Asparagus, celery, parsley, basil, carrots, chives, marigolds
Turnips	Peas
Wallflowers	Apples
Zucchini	Nasturtiums

Bad Companions

Alliums*	Peas, beans
Apples	Grass, potatoes
Artichoke	Legumes
Beans	Onions, garlic, fennel, gladioli, sunflowers
Brassicas*	Strawberries
Broccoli	Strawberries
Cabbage	Rue
Carrots	Tomatoes
Carnations	Hyacinths
Cauliflowers	Strawberries
Coriander	Fennel
Corn	Wheat, oats, rye
Cucurbits*	Potatoes
Eggplant	Potatoes
Fennel	Beans, tomatoes, kohlrabi, coriander, wormwood
Garlic	Peas, beans, cabbage, strawberries

Gladioli	Strawberries, beans, peas
Hyssop	Radishes
Kohlrabi	Tomatoes, beans
Mint	Parsley, parsnip carrots, celery, cabbages
Peas	Onions, shallots, garlic
Potatoes	Apples, cherries, cucumbers, pumpkins, sunflowers, tomatoes, raspberries, rosemary
Pumpkins	Potatoes
Radishes	Hyssop
Raspberries	Blackberries, potatoes
Rue	Sage, basil
Strawberries	Cabbages, cauliflowers, Brussels sprouts, gladioli, tomatoes
Sunflowers	Potatoes
Tomatoes	Rosemary, potatoes, kohlrabi, fennel, apricots

* alliums = onions, leeks, garlic, chives, shalloots, green onions, potatoes, onions

* brassicas = cabbage, caulifower, Brussels sprouts, broccoli, kale, collards,
   Chinese cabbage, pak choie, turnips, mustard

*cucurbits= gourds, melons, pumpkins, squash, cucumbers

God almighty first planted a garden. And indeed, it is the purest of human pleasures.

~Francis Bacon

....

chapter 6

Maintaining a Companion Garden

BANANA SKINS

The skin of the banana is surprisingly rich in calcium, sodium, silica, sulfur, magnesium, and phosphates. Tucking banana skins under the topsoil around rosebushes or geraniums is one of the simplest and quickest ways of providing valuable plant food.

BEER

Beer can provide nourishment to plants. The rinsings of empty beer bottles will be appreciated by indoor plants, plants in tubs, and border flowers.

COMPOST

Making compost is one of the joys of gardening. Finding kitchen waste, old newspapers, grass clippings, garden cuttings, vacuum cleaner fluff, etc., transformed into crumbly black soil is enormously satisfying. If you are dubious about putting something into the compost bin, just ask yourself if it's ever been alive—if it has, it's okay to put in.

You can buy a compost bin or make your own. In each case, the bottom layer must be on the ground. If you don't want to buy or to construct a combost bin, you can at least pile all your waste in a hidden corner of the garden, observing the rule of a thinnish layer of waste alternating with a scattering of earth, and an occasional scattering of lime and fertilizer. A properly constructed compost heap is, of course, more sanitary, and results are more quickly achieved.

But if you feel you just can't be bothered, at least do yourself the favor of not burning waste but of piling it, out of sight and out of smell range. The results will probably convince you that it's worth taking more trouble next time. Most gardening books give a blow-by-blow description of how to construct your own compost pile. I swear by the bought plastic bins and even more by compost, which acts as a life-infusion to the garden.

CROP ROTATION

It is a mistake to grow the same plant family in the same spot year after year. Continuous demand for the same type of nutriment will eventually render the soil too impoverished to be of use.

An ideal arrangement is:

a. Fertilize the soil with manured compost.

b. Plant in it heavy feeders, such as cabbage, cauliflowers, celery, leeks, sweet corn, squash, cucumbers, spinach, lettuce, and endive.

c. The following year use the space for beans or peas. Vegetables from the legume family put nitrogen back into the soil.

d. The third year plant light feeders, such as carrots, beets, radishes, parsnips, or turnips where the legumes have been.

e. Start the process over again.

FERTILIZERS

Rinsed-out milk bottles, beer bottles, teapots, and any vegetable water you may have are all valuable. Pot-plants grown on windowsills are grateful for such small mercies.

HERB TEAS

To prepare herb "teas" for spraying garden plants, follow these general directions: cover the selected amount of herbs with water, bring the water to the boil for a minute or two, then remove the pan from the heat and strain the water off. Dilute the tea with 4 times the amount of water and use at once. The sludgy mess left behind  can be added to the compost bin. When making herb teas, it is best to use the younger leaves of the plant. Once a plant has blossomed, the leaves have lost most of their strength.

Some herbs require a different treatment. These tea recipes will be found under their individual headings.

LEAVES

The fallen leaf can be a gardener's bane or blessing, depending on the gardener's attitude. Wise gardeners lust after fallen leaves and, without any of their own, will travel in pursuit of the free bounty. Layers of leaves are a must for the compost bin, but they should be shredded before you use them as a mulch. (A layer of solid leaves can make it tough going for plants trying to push their way to the light.) If you don't have a machine that chops your compost but you want to use dead leaves as mulch, run the garden mower over them, backwards and forwards, until they are of a consistency fine enough to be run through spread fingers.

MILDEW

Many plants, such as begonias, are subject to mildew. Dried sage sprinkled around the plants will help, as will spraying with teas made from horsetail or nettle.

MONOCULTURE

The planting of a mass of one species is a mistake. It's like lining up the silver in one place to make it easy for the burglar. Mixed plantings make for mutual protection. Plants that keep their roots near the surface should be planted next to those that root deeply. Two plant varieties that both need a great deal of moisture should not be planted together, as they will need to fight for what is available.

Monoculture is the most common mistake made by gardeners. There is nothing that attracts pests more than the prospect of rich and easy feeding and, once ensconced, the pests multiply like mad.

MULCHES

Many gardeners swear that a no-work garden is achieved by using mulch. Mulches are fine, as far as they go. But a mulch on poor soil is going to take a devil of a time to bring it up to scratch, so before applying a mulch of chopped leaves or hay or straw, it is as well to do your best for the soil underneath by giving it compost. Mulches keep down weeds and, when decomposed, add life to the soil, but aesthetics enter into gardening and many people do not enjoy seeing their plants growing above anything but brown soil or green ground cover. I believe in mulches, but I like them concealed by soil. There is nothing pleasing about the sight of chopped newspaper or spiky hay between rows of growing plants. Leaves used as mulch should be shredded to give a porous blanket through which seedlings may push.

NEWSPAPER

Newspaper is made from wood pulp and is degradable. It can be shredded and added to the compost bin or used directly on the soil. Overlapping thicknesses of newspaper, well soaked, can go into the bottom of trenches and can be used as a layer below mulches of leaves to keep down weeds. Newspaper can then go back to the soil from which it grew.

NICOTINE

Nicotine makes a great spray against scale pests and mealy bugs. You can either purchase a nicotine spray or soak cigarette butts in water to make your own, thereby easing your conscience about smoking. Thirty cigarette or cigar butts soaked in 1 gallon (4.5 L) of water for five days will make an effective brew. Be careful not to use nicotine spray near tomatoes, as the nicotine spray can spread disease among them.

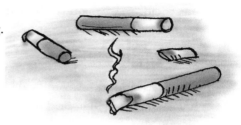

PEPPER

When shaken around plants, black pepper will protect them against animals and some insects. Sprinkled on dew-wet leaves, pepper will keep caterpillars away.

QUASSIA

A spray made from quassia chips is good against caterpillars and aphids, and it won't kill the ladybugs that live on the aphids. You can buy quassia chips at most health-food stores.

Put one tablespoon of quassia chips in a quart (1 L) of water, bring to a boil, and simmer for two hours. Then dilute the liquid with five times the amount of water for use against aphids, and four times the amount of water if you are up against caterpillars.

ROTENONE

Rotenone dust, made from the roots of the derris plant, is a "safe" insecticide to use against chewing and sucking insects. It is harmless to humans and plants, but can poison fish, so don't use it near a pond.

SALT

If red spider mites and cabbage worms are extra troublesome, a hot salt spray will get rid of them and, surprisingly, won't harm the plants. A heaped tablespoon of salt dissolved in 1 gallon (4.5 L) of hot water is the strength recommended, but it would be as well to soak the ground well afterwards to disperse the salt, as it could damage young and tender roots.

You can kill snails and slugs by putting salt on them, but there are less messy methods.

SEAWEED

Seaweed, a good source of potash, makes a marvelous fertilizer. Collect seaweed from the beach, wash it well when you get it home, and add it to the compost bin—not as one great blanket, but in judiciously thin layers.

Seaweed spray is helpful in fighting insect infestations. When sprayed on a plant or tree, the liquid dries and smothers the eggs and larvae of insects. When you peel off the spray, all the pests come with it.

To make this spray, boil about 18 ounces (500 g) seaweed in 4.5 gallons (20 L) of water (you can, of course, make proportionally less) for an hour or until a lesser amount thickens.

SOAP

A soapy spray is made by dissolving 8 ounces (225 g) common laundry soap (not liquid detergent) in 2 gallons (9 L) of water. After spraying plants, hose them down with clean water and repeat the two processes as often as necessary.

TEA LEAVES

Tea leaves are appreciated by both camellias and geraniums—in the soil around them, not over them. Tea leaves are also helpful to citrus fruit trees.

TRAPS

Place broad leaves or pieces of cardboard daubed with molasses on the ground at night. These will attract and trap pests that can be easily disposed of in the morning.

Leave pieces of raw potato and carrot where you want to trap wireworms.

Leave a bucket of water under an outside light to trap moths and many other types of flying insects.

When left upside down in the garden, lettuce leaves, spinach leaves, or orange or grapefruit cups will attract night-feeders who will be found there sleeping the next day.

Small, shallow containers of sugar water, honey, beer, dried yeast, etc., will trap many pests while you sleep.

VIRUS

Whole, lowfat, or nonfat milk makes a good spray for use on plants that show signs of viral disease. If using dried milk, dissolve about 18 ounces (500 g) in 1 gallon (4.5 L) of water.

WATER

A good, hard jet of water will blast away aphids quite successfully. A dousing with hot water can get rid of other types of pests and is unlikely to hurt the plants. But don't use boiling water.

WOOD ASH

Spread between garden rows, wood ash helps protect plants from a variety of pests.

A light sprinkling of wood ash around cauliflower, onions, beets, turnips, peas, and lettuce plants will be beneficial.

INDEX*

A

Ajuga 58

Alfalfa 45, 47

Alliums 104, 105, 108, 109

Annual herbs 59, 67

Ants 23-25, 49, 54, 55, 65, 75, 82, 94

Aphids 23-26, 29, 33, 34, 37, 42, 48, 52, 65,
        69, 73, 76-79, 85, 86, 89, 99, 117

Apples 7, 45-47, 57, 64, 65, 76, 98, 104, 105

Apricots 32, 47, 49, 74, 103, 109

Asparagus 20, 48, 79, 103, 106

Asters 48

B

Bark 32, 39, 41

Basil 10, 20, 25, 26, 31, 32, 36, 47-49, 66,
        73, 87, 95, 103, 105, 107, 109

Bay 38, 48, 49

Beans 7, 10, 15-17, 19, 20, 24, 28, 34, 49-52,
        55, 59, 60, 63, 64, 69, 70, 80-82,
        92, 103-109

Beer 40, 111, 120

Bees 26, 59, 63, 69, 71, 75, 79, 81, 84, 86,
        91, 92, 95

Beetles 26, 30, 34, 35, 37, 39, 74, 79, 82, 83

Beets 16, 17, 19, 20, 50-52, 69, 71, 72, 78,
        93, 103-107, 113, 120

Birds 7, 27, 34, 37, 41, 67, 76, 83, 92, 93

Blight 82, 84

Borage 21, 26, 51

Brassicas 15, 20, 104, 109

Broccoli 16, 17, 51, 53, 70, 77, 82, 91, 106,
        109

Bulbs 36, 66, 97

Butterflies 27

C

Cabbage 7, 16, 17, 50-53, 55, 56, 59, 60,
        63-65, 68, 69, 75, 79, 82, 85, 86,
        88-91, 93-96, 104-106, 108, 109

Calcium 59, 87, 90, 111

Camellias 53, 119

Carnations 54

Carrots 15-17, 19, 20, 24, 46, 47, 50, 53-55,
        57, 59, 62, 70, 71, 78, 80, 81, 88,
        89, 95, 103-109

Caterpillars 26-28, 33, 37, 41, 42, 65, 66, 69,
        75, 97, 117

Catmint 36, 55, 58

Cauliflower 16, 17, 28, 50, 53, 55, 77, 91, 104, 106, 109, 113, 120

Celery 15-18, 20, 37, 52, 55, 56, 60, 70, 80, 90, 95, 104, 105, 107, 109, 113

Centipedes 28

Chamomile 20, 36, 52, 56, 57, 85, 93, 96, 104

Chervil 57, 59, 104, 106

Citrus trees 58

Clubroot 52, 85

Comfrey 58, 59

Companion Crops 18, 93

Companion

garden 5, 11, 13, 14, 111

herbs 14

Companion planting 5, 7, 9-11, 73

Companion plants 5, 10, 23, 45, 82, 90, 98, 100

Compost heap 30, 39, 56, 57, 62, 77, 78, 92, 94, 98, 100, 112-114, 116, 118

Coriander 26, 57, 59, 62, 63, 104, 108

Crops 10, 14-17, 36, 50, 58-60, 67, 77, 78, 83, 90, 92, 100, 105

Cucumbers 16-18, 50, 51, 59-61, 71, 77, 81, 82, 88, 90, 92, 100, 104, 106, 107, 109, 113

Cutworms 28, 29, 41, 42, 51, 52, 55, 94, 96

D

Dandelions 45, 61, 62

Dill 20, 21, 37, 52, 55, 57, 59, 62, 63, 104

Disease 23, 25, 49, 51, 57, 60, 117, 120

Disinfectant 95, 99

E

Earthworms 30, 42, 93, 98

Earwigs 30, 37

Eau-de-cologne mint 31

Eelworms 31, 61, 74, 83

Eggplants 83, 94, 105, 108

Eggs 33, 38, 42, 52, 72, 118

F

Fennel 20, 21, 26, 31, 50, 59, 62-64, 95, 99, 108, 109

Fertilizer 59, 61, 77, 100, 112

Fleas 31, 63, 93, 99

Flowers 7, 27, 31, 42, 43, 48, 56, 57, 62-64, 69, 72-75, 88, 91, 93, 97, 99

Flying insects 29, 38, 94, 119

Foxgloves 47, 103

Fruit 32, 47-49, 73, 76, 80, 89, 91, 92

    fly 32, 80, 89

    trees 45, 67, 70, 71, 89, 97, 99, 105, 119

Fungus 67, 68

G

Garlic 15, 16, 19, 21, 24, 25, 28, 48, 50, 64,
        65, 80, 81, 84, 86, 87, 105, 106,
        108, 109

Geraniums 66, 111, 119

Green manure 15-17

H

Herb Teas 25, 28, 40, 46, 61, 67, 77, 99, 100,
        114

Herbs 10, 14, 20, 21, 24, 25, 47, 51, 52, 57,
        59, 67, 68, 70, 79, 82, 87, 88, 94,
        114

Horseradish 67

Horsetail 46, 48, 67, 68, 103, 115

Hoverflies 33, 75, 78, 80, 92

Hyacinths 54

Hyssop 52, 68, 90, 96, 105, 109

I

Insecticide 84, 118

Insects 11, 23, 25, 27, 29, 32, 39, 41-43, 53,
        56, 57, 72, 75-77, 87, 91, 117, 118

    eggs 33,38,42,52,72,118

    larvae 27, 29, 33, 42, 53, 118

Iron 77, 90

K

Kennel 63

Kohlrabi 50, 63, 69, 77, 95, 104-106, 108,
        109

L

Lacewings 33, 37, 92

Ladybugs 11, 25, 34, 35, 100, 117

Larkspur 69

Lavender 54, 58, 69, 84, 96, 107

Leeks 16, 53-56, 70, 104, 109, 113

Legumes 10, 70, 113

Lemon 59, 74, 90, 94

Lizards 35

Loganberries 82, 84

M

Maggots 54, 55, 78

Marigolds 72, 74, 96

Mealybugs 33

Melons 36, 58, 59, 90, 92, 107, 109

Mildew 51, 53, 57, 61, 68, 77, 88, 115

Millipedes 36

Mint 21, 36, 37, 52, 56, 75, 79, 88, 96, 101, 104, 109

Moths 36, 37, 89, 94, 99

Mulch layer 59

N

Nasturtiums 21, 47, 54, 76, 77, 83, 84, 100, 101, 106

Nettles 25, 77, 78, 81, 83, 96, 115

Newspaper 112, 116

Nicotine 25, 97, 116, 117

O

Oats 15, 47, 49, 108

Onions 10, 15-17, 36, 45, 50, 52-54, 56, 69-71, 78, 80, 86, 87, 89, 90, 93, 104-107, 109

P

Parsley 15, 21, 48, 50, 57, 59, 75, 79, 80, 86, 95, 96, 103, 104, 106, 107

Parsnips 15, 17, 80, 113

Peas 15-17, 19, 21, 49, 50, 54, 59, 64, 66, 70, 80-82, 84, 90, 92, 104-106, 108, 109

Peppers 27, 28, 59, 66, 80, 106, 117

Peppermint 20, 37

Pests 5, 7, 11, 23, 25, 31-35, 41, 43, 48-50, 52, 59, 60, 63, 92, 115, 116, 120

Plants
    aphid-ridden 25
    aromatic 85, 99
    edible 47
    shallow-rooted 45
    susceptible 50

Pollen 91

Pollination 26

Potassium 59, 70, 93, 94

Potato 9, 14, 21, 46, 47, 50, 52, 59, 60, 64, 67, 70, 74, 77, 80-84, 92, 104-109

Praying mantis 29, 37

Pumpkins 10, 82, 83, 90, 109

Pyrethrum 24, 25, 83, 84, 92, 97

R

Raspberries 82, 84, 85, 93, 107, 109

Red spider mites 38, 48, 65, 75, 78, 118

Rhubarb 52, 84, 85

Rosemary 20, 21, 37, 52, 55, 86, 95, 96, 104, 109

Roses 65, 74, 78-80, 86-89, 93, 97, 106, 107, 111

Rotation 14

Rue 49, 87

Russian Garlic 47, 53

Rye 15, 16, 49, 108

S

Sage 20, 21, 37, 47, 52-55, 58, 75, 86-88, 91, 96, 99, 104

Salt 118

Scale insects 33, 34, 42

Scents 10, 24, 47, 52, 56, 72, 80

Seedlings 15-19, 28, 116

Shrubs 88, 95, 97

Slugs 39, 40, 67, 78, 87, 90, 99, 118

Snails 26, 35, 39-41, 78, 118

Soap 25, 38, 65, 119

Soil 7, 14, 30, 45, 50, 51, 54, 55, 59, 60, 70, 77, 78, 81, 86, 87, 90-93, 96-98, 112, 113, 115, 116

Southernwood 20, 24, 32, 36, 47, 52, 73, 89, 96, 103

Sowing 10, 13

Soybeans 90

Spearmint 36, 97

Spiders 37, 41, 65

Spinach 50, 90, 91, 104, 107, 113, 120

Squash 15, 83, 91, 92, 107, 109, 113

Stinging nettles 36, 47

Strawberries 24, 51, 52, 55, 64, 66, 71, 91, 92, 104, 105, 108, 109

Summer Grouping 18

Sun 11, 14, 35, 87, 98

Sunflowers 50, 60, 82, 92, 93, 105, 108, 109

Swiss chard 15-17, 50, 78, 93, 104, 106

T

Tansy 21, 24, 28, 29, 31, 32, 36, 37, 47, 52, 58, 80, 84, 93, 94, 103

Tarragon 94

Tea 25, 46, 53, 57, 67, 68, 77, 79, 98, 114, 115, 119

Thistles 94

Thrips 33, 42, 69, 78

Thyme 20, 26, 37, 52, 53, 88, 94-96, 104

Toads 42

Tomatoes 9, 10, 15-18, 21, 48, 52, 59, 62-65,
              69, 71, 74, 75, 78, 82, 95-97, 103,
              105-109

Topsoil 111

Trees 46, 54, 57, 66, 76, 78, 80, 81, 89, 97,
              118

Tulips 97

Turnips 69, 77, 81, 84, 97, 106, 109, 113, 120

U

Underplant 47, 58

V

Vegetables 14, 31, 59, 80, 81, 100, 113

W

Wallflowers 46, 98, 103, 107

Wasps 42, 43, 75, 90, 92, 100

Whiteflies 34, 48, 49

Wood ash 40, 55, 72, 78, 82, 97, 120

Wormwood 20, 25, 40, 55, 58, 84, 99, 108

Y

Yarrow 84, 99, 100

Z

Zucchini 90, 100, 101